the

LAVA

of

this

LAND

TRIQUARTERLY BOOKS
NORTHWESTERN UNIVERSITY PRESS

Evanston, Illinois

SOUTH

AFRICAN

POETRY

1960–1996

the

LAVA

of

this

LAND

edited by DENIS HIRSON

TriQuarterly Books

Northwestern University Press

Evanston, Illinois 60208-4210

Compilation copyright © 1997 by TriQuarterly Books/Northwestern University Press

Published 1997 All rights reserved

Printed in the United States of America

ISBN 0-8101-5068-9 (cloth)

ISBN 0-8101-5069-7 (paper)

Library of Congress Cataloging-in-Publication Data

The lava of this land   South African poetry, 1960–1996 / edited by Denis Hirson
        p   cm
    Poems in English with some translations from Afrikaans, Xam, Xhosa, and Zulu
    ISBN 0-8101-5068-9 (cloth   alk   paper) — ISBN 0-8101-5069-7 (paper   alk   paper)
    1 South African poetry—20th century—Translations into English 2 South African poetry
(English)—20th century I Hirson, Denis
PL8014 S62L38 1997
809' 8968—dc21   97-15916
                                                              CIP

The paper used in this publication meets the minimum requirements of the American National

Standard for Information Sciences—Permanence of Paper for Printed Library Materials,

ANSI Z39 48-1984

CONTENTS

Acknowledgements   xiii

Introduction   xvii

SECTION I

Stephen Watson

Song of the Broken String   3

Our Blood Makes Smoke   4

Rain in a Dead Man's Footsteps   5

The Rain that Is Male   6

The Sound of the Stars   7

The Sun, the Moon and the Knife   7

The Nature of /Kaggen   8

Sydney Clouts

Firebowl   10

Hotknife   11

Stick Song   12

North Wind   12

Within   13

After the Riot   14

Poetry Is Death Cast Out   14

Ingrid Jonker

"I went searching for the way of my body . . . "   15

Tokoloshe   15

Bitterberry Daybreak   16

Pregnant Woman   16

Homesickness for Cape Town   18

The Child Who Was Shot Dead by Soldiers in Nyanga   18

Sob. W. Nkuhlu

The Land of the People Once Living   20

St. J. Page Yako

The Contraction and Enclosure of the Land   24

Dennis Brutus

Nightsong: City   25

Cold   25

Arthur Nortje

Waiting   27

Adam Small

Come, Let Us Sing   29

from Great Krismis Prayer   30

Preacher   31

On the P'rade   32

Gesondheid!   33

Five quatrains from Black Bronze Beautiful   34

SECTION II
_____

Mongane Wally Serote

Alexandra   39

City Johannesburg   40

I Will Wait   41

Ofay-Watcher Looks Back   42

For Don M – Banned   43

Milk and Corn   43

Hell, Well, Heaven   44

Two extracts from No Baby Must Weep   45

Breyten Breytenbach

"I will die and go to my father . . . "   49

my heritage   50

"how drowsy we were wrapped in coolness . . . "   51

the truth   52

plagiarism   53

your letter   55

december   56

for Françooi Viljoen   59

Wopko Jensma

Spanner in the What? Works   61

Cry Me a River   62

Our King   63

My Hands   64

Confidentially Yours   64

Now That It's Too Late   66

My Brother   67

Joburg Spiritual   68

Eva Bezwoda

"A tooth dressed up in jackboots . . . "   71

"Sometimes the mouth's a locked cell . . . "   71

The Bullet   72

Villages   72

Ice Floes   73

"He lay with her . . . "   73

Njabulo S. Ndebele

Be Gentle   75

The Revolution of the Aged   75

The Man of Smoke   77

Mbuyiseni Oswald Mtshali

Boy on a Swing   81

Men in Chains   81

Amagoduka at Glencoe Station   82

The Detribalised   85

Talismans   88

Mandla Langa

The Pension Jiveass   90

Mazisi Kunene

Death of the Miners *or* The Widows of the Earth   91

The Political Prisoner   92

The Tyrant   93

A Note to All Surviving Africans   94

To My Friend Solomon Hailu   94

Sheila Cussons

Clothed Nakedness   96

Organ   96

The Barn-Yard   97

Yellow Gramophone   98

Pearl   98

Wilma Stockenström

Africa Love   100

East Coast   100

Koichab's Water   101

The Rock   101

Confession of a Glossy Starling   103

The Skull Laughs though the Face Cries   104

Housebreaking of the Mamba   105

Jeni Couzyn

 Three sections from Christmas in Africa 106

SECTION III

Oupa Thando Mthimkulu

 Like a Wheel 117

 Nineteen Seventy-Six 117

Motshile Nthodi

 Staffrider 119

 South African Dialogue 122

K. Zwide

 Wooden Spoon 125

Sipho Sepamla

 Da Same, Da Same 126

Mafika Gwala

 Gumba, Gumba, Gumba 128

 Bonk'abajahile 131

 Kwela-Ride 134

 Tap-Tapping 134

 One Small Boy Longs for Summer 135

Chris van Wyk

 It Is Sleepy in the "Coloured" Townships 137

 Candle 138

 The Road 139

 We Can't Meet Here, Brother 140

 In Detention 140

 A Riot Policeman 141

Peter Horn

 The Eruption of Langa, 30th March 1960 143

Stephen Gray

 Local History 144

 Song of the Gold Coming In 144

Patrick Cullinan

 To Have Love 147

 The First, Far Beat 147

 The Dust in the Wind 147

North   148

Sir Tom   149

Etruscan Girl   151

Don Maclennan

Letters   154

"Winter sunlight, clean as a cut orange . . . "   155

Funeral III   155

Douglas Livingstone

Gentling a Wildcat   157

A Piece of Earth   159

Mpondo's Smithy, Transkei   160

SECTION IV

Jeremy Cronin

"To learn how to speak . . . "   163

"Our land holds . . . "   164

White Face, Black Mask   165

Poem-Shrike   166

Motho ke Motho ka Batho Babang   167

Walking on Air   168

I Saw Your Mother   176

Your Deep Hair   177

Gcina Mhlophe

The Dancer   178

Douglas Reid Skinner

The Body Is a Country of Joy and Pain   180

Law and Order   182

Donald Parenzee

The Raining   185

Interview   185

Changes at the Settlement   186

Andries Walter Oliphant

Childhood in Heidelberg   188

Poem for My Mother   189

After Life   190

Song of the Unemployed   191

The Hunger Striker   192

Blue   193

Ingrid de Kok

Small Passing   195

Our Sharpeville   197

Sun, Aloe, Rain   198

To Drink Its Water   200

This Thing We Learn from Others   201

Brush Stroke   202

Inner Note   203

Ground Wave   204

Stephen Watson

North-West Cape, 1985   205

Descending, Late   205

Phil du Plessis

Easter Transit   208

Petra Müller

Three sections from Foretelling   209

Antjie Krog

Ma   211

Song of the Cyclists   211

a one-dimensional song for the northern free state, more
specifically middenspruit   213

lovesong after the music of K. E. Ntsane   214

"I don't glance at your grizzled hair . . . "   215

transparency of the sole   216

refused march at Kroonstad Monday 23 Oct 1989   218

land   219

Karen Press

Dispossessed Words   220

Tikolosh   222

Statues   222

Heart's Hunger   223

Needlework   227

The First Thirty-Seven Years   227

Can't Stand, Can't Dance   228

from Tiresias in the City of Heroes   228

Robert Berold

Dark City   231

Two Meditations on Chuang Tsu   231

Praise Poem   233

There Is a River in Me   234

meet me   234

Those Days   235

Kelwyn Sole

Poem from Botswana   236

Presence   237

Mankunku   239

The National Question   239

Woman, Trespassing in a Garden   240

Homecoming   242

Housing Targets   243

SECTION V

Tatamkhulu Afrika

Tamed   247

The Funeral of Anton Fransch   250

The Trap   252

The Mugging   254

Who Were You?   256

Cat on a High Yard Wall   257

Remembering   259

Solitary Child   260

Nightrider   261

Joan Metelerkamp

Sunday Night – On My Own – After the Uitenhage
Shootings   263

Trees Sky Space   264

Dove   265

Lisa Combrinck

Ghazal   268

In the Moonlight   269

Cathy Zerbst

       Magnolia Blue   270

Johann de Lange

       Koos Prinsloo [1957–1994]   271

Ari Sitas

       Evening Tides I   274

       Ethekwini   274

       Six sections from Slave Trades   276

Sandile Dikeni

       Track of the Tracks   282

Rustum Kozain

       Family Portrait   285

       from Brother, Who Will Bury Me?   286

Mxolisi M. Nyezwa

       barracks   288

       things change   288

       I cannot think of all the pains   289

Lesego Rampolokeng

       After Bra W's Flowers   291

       In Transition   292

       For the Oral   294

       Wet pain . . . tread with care   296

Seitlhamo Motsapi

       shak-shak   297

       enia   298

       sol/o   299

       mushi   300

       the sun used to be white   301

       missa joe   303

       river robert   304

Appendix   307

Explanatory Notes   311

Glossary   314

Biographical Notes   319

ACKNOWLEDGEMENTS

This anthology would never have seen the light of day without the close collaboration of Robert Berold; the poems that have appeared in *New Coin* magazine under his inspired editorship gave me the initial impulse to put *The Lava of This Land* together, and his generous help and critical comments have been indispensable from start to finish.

Ansie Cilliers has nourished this anthology in several ways: helping to sift through Afrikaans poems, screening translations, and providing the backbone for the explanatory notes and glossary. Colleen Higgs came up with a mine of information for the biographical notes.

Thanks for collaboration on translations are due to Johann de Lange, Mike Dickman, Karen Press, and James Munnick.

For dialogues, comments, and midwifing skills, I'd like to thank Adine Sagalyn, Antjie Krog, Ellen Hinsey, and Professor Edgard Sienaert.

Lastly, I greatly appreciated the warm and enthusiastic response to this project from Fernando Ainsa of UNESCO Publishing and Reginald Gibbons of TriQuarterly Books; Reginald Gibbons gave me unfailing support during its production.

For permission to use previously published work in this volume, grateful acknowledgement is made to the following: *New Coin*, The Carrefour Press, Snailpress, and the author for poems by Tatamkhulu Afrika; *West Coast Line*, Bateleur Press, The Carrefour Press, and the author for poems by Robert Berold; Robert Royston, Lionel Abrahams of Renoster Books, and Workbench for poems by Eva Bezwoda; John Calder, Faber and Faber, and the author for poems by Breyten Breytenbach, Denis Hirson for his revised translations of Breytenbach's "I will die and go to my father . . . ," "how drowsy we were wrapped in coolness . . . ," and "plagiarism"; Heinemann Educational Books and the author for poems by

Dennis Brutus; Purnell, David Philip, and Marjorie Clouts for the Estate of Sydney Clouts for his poems; *New Coin* and the author for poems by Lisa Combrinck; Heinemann Educational Books and the author for poems by Jeni Couzyn; Snailpress and the author for poems by Patrick Cullinan; Tafelberg Press, Amanda Botha Enterprises, and the author for poems by Sheila Cussons, Penguin Books for Johann de Lange's translation of "The Barn-Yard," and Johann de Lange for his translation of "Clothed Nakedness"; *New Coin, New Contrast,* Ravan Press, Penguin Books, and the author for poems by Ingrid de Kok; Johann de Lange for the translation of his poem "Koos Prinsloo [1957–1994]"; *TriQuarterly* and the author for the poem by Phil du Plessis; *New Contrast* and the author for the poem by Sandile Dikeni; David Philip and the author for poems by Stephen Gray; Ad Donker Publishers, Ravan Press, and the author for poems by Mafika Gwala; Scribe Press, Ravan Press, and the author for the poem by Peter Horn; Ravan Press for poems by Wopko Jensma, Ansie Cilliers and Karen Press for their translation of "Now That It's Too Late," Karen Press for her translation of "Our King"; Human and Rousseau and the Estate of Ingrid Jonker for her poems, Penguin Books and Cherry Clayton for her translation of "Bitterberry Daybreak"; *New Coin,* Penguin Books, and the author for poems by Rustum Kozain; Human and Rousseau, Taurus, Hond, and the author for poems by Antjie Krog; *TriQuarterly* for Jane Taylor, David Bunn, and the author's translation of "Lovesong After the Music of K. E. Ntsane," *World Literature Today* and Karen Press for her transla- tions of "refused march at Kroonstad Monday 23 Oct 1989" and "land," Karen Press for her translations of "Ma" and "Song of the "Cyclists," Denis Hirson for his translations of "a one-dimensional song for the northern free state, more specifically middenspruit," "I don't glance at your grizzled hair," and "transparency of the sole"; *TriQuarterly, World Literature Today,* Heinemann Educational Books, Allen & Unwin, Ravan Press, and the author for poems by Masizi Kunene; Ad Donker Publishers and the author for the

poem by Mandla Langa; Ad Donker Publishers and the Estate of
Douglas Livingstone for his poems; The Carrefour Press, Snailpress,
and the author for poems by Don Maclennan; The Carrefour
Press, Gecko Books, and the author for poems by Joan
Metelerkamp; Gcina Mhlophe for her poem; Deep South
Publishers, The Institute for the Study of English in Africa, and the
author for poems by Seitlhamo Motsapi; *Staffrider* and the author
for poems by Oupa Thando Mthimkulu; Lionel Abrahams of
Renoster Books, Oxford University Press, Shuter and Shooter, and
Ad Donker Publications for poems by Mbuyiseni Oswald Mtshali;
New Coin and the author for poems by Petra Müller; *The Classic,
Contrast, Staffrider,* and the author for poems by Njabulo S.
Ndebele; Perskor for the poem by Sob. W. Nkuhlu, *Ophir* and
Ravan Press for its translation by Robert Kavanagh and Z. S.
Qangule; Ravan Press for poems by Motshile Nthodi; Heinemann
Educational Books and the UNISA Library for the poem by Arthur
Nortje; *New Coin,* The Congress of South African Writers, and the
author for poems by Mxolisi M. Nyezwa; *New Coin, New Contrast,*
Justified Press, Dangaroo Press, and the author for poems by
Andries Walter Oliphant; Ravan Press and the author for poems by
Donald Parenzee; *New Coin, New Contrast,* The Cinnamon
Crocodile, and the author for poems by Karen Press; *New Coin,*
COSAW Publications, and the author for poems by Lesego
Rampolokeng; Ad Donker Publications and the author for poems
by Mongane Wally Serote; Ad Donker Publications and the author
for the poem by Sipho Sepamla; *New Coin,* COSAW Publications,
and the author for poems by Ari Sitas; The Carrefour Press and
the author for poems by Douglas Reid Skinner; Holandsch
Afrikaansche Uitgewers Maatschappij, Ad Donker Publications,
and the author for poems by Adam Small, Mike Dickman for his
translations of "Come, Let Us Sing," "Great Krismis Prayer,"
"Preacher," and "On the P'rade"; *The South African Review of
Books,* Ravan Press, and the author for poems by Kelwyn Sole;
Human and Rousseau, Reijeruitgewers, and the author for poems

by Wilma Stockenström, Bloomsbury Publishing Ltd. for Johann de Lange's translation of "Africa Love," Johann de Lange for his translations of "East Coast," "Koichab's Water," "The Rock," "Confession of a Glossy Starling," "The Skull Laughs though the Face Cries," and "Housebreaking of the Mamba"; *Staffrider, New Coin, TriQuarterly,* Ad Donker Publications, and the author for poems by Chris van Wyk; The Carrefour Press, The Sheepmeadow Press, and the author for poems by Stephen Watson; Perskor for the poem by St. J. Page Yako, *Ophir* and Ravan Press for its translation by Robert Kavanagh and Z. S. Qangule; *New Coin* and the author for the poem by Cathy Zerbst; *Staffrider* and Ravan Press for the poem by K. Zwide.

"South African poetry" meant something quite specific to many readers not so very long ago: a momentary flame of words in the sombre confinement of apartheid, a sign that not everyone had been snuffed out by the pig-iron hand and airless language of oppression.

Yet South African poetry has always been highly diverse, rooted in both African and European traditions, reflecting what has until recently been a ruthlessly divided society.

In terms of written poetry, this diversity has never been more apparent than over the past fifteen years or so, as the country has slowly, with great and violent difficulty, woken to a new dispensation. Poets have considerably widened the frontiers of their work, writing poems that go off like firecrackers as different kinds of languages are compounded together and ignited; poems in which social dream and disillusionment together feed uneasy tight-knuckled metaphors; poems that twine tales of South Africa's poverty-struck wasteland into lean lines down the page; poems that risk their skin in descriptions of intense intimacy; poems in which memory of the past cools the molten violence of the present; poems that no longer find themselves living on an island at the end of a continent; poems whose raw music throbs at the edge of change.

Such poems contain something of the recent, deep news from South Africa. It was their striking appearance in print which fuelled what I felt to be the growing necessity for this anthology. Yet, at the same time, this work cannot be separated from a body of South African poetry dating back primarily to the early 1960s, poetry whose power is still very much alive today.

In exploring the relationship between poems written over the past four decades, I have found it necessary to divide this anthology into five sections, roughly representing the following time periods: early 1960s to late 1960s; early 1970s to 1976; post-1976 to the

A period review of the anthology

early 1980s; mid-1980s to 1996; 1990 to 1996. (For specific dates of publication, see the appendix.) The poems in each section may be read together as a constellation, whether for the resonance they share or for the spark struck by the dissonance between them. To this end I have sometimes juggled with the exact chronological order in which poets, and their work, appear.

Most poems here were either originally written in English or translated from the Afrikaans. The razor wire of the linguistic divide, a legacy of the apartheid years, still lies thickly coiled across the territory of South African letters; the translation of poetry generally remains a stunted art, more particularly when it comes to poetry in African languages.[1] Partly as a result, I have found few poems in these languages which fall within the scope of this anthology. Apart from the poems by Stephen Watson, "versions" of Bushman narratives which open this anthology, I have included poems by Sob. W. Nkuhlu and St. J. Page Yako (originally in Xhosa) and Mazisi Kunene (originally in Zulu).

Translated recordings of oral literature have been excluded. Although some of these are particularly fine,[2] they are for the most part composed for theatrical performance, dependent on an audience which would implicitly share local references. This anthology comprises poems originally destined for the relative autonomy of the written page, though a good number may seem to rise up tremoring from their silent rectangle to meet the eardrum; in some cases, this is due to the direct influence of oral poetry upon the writer.

These remarks point to the limits of this anthology and once again emphasize the extreme diversity of poets in South Africa. Yet I have situated the centre of gravity of this anthology away from any lethal fray between them, in the ground of the country which all of them here speak out of and/or about. Without wishing to reduce the highly varied work of the fifty-four poets represented here to the shape of any single mould, I would suggest that they, amongst others, nonetheless contribute to a loosely defined lineage of autochthonous South African written poetry.

J. M. Coetzee, discussing the poetry of Sydney Clouts, points to the way in which he breaks with his South African English-language predecessors, from Thomas Pringle onwards, "who have described Africa as . . . a mere negative reflection or shadow of Europe, insubstantial."[3] Clouts, on the contrary, provides a "radical response to the burden of finding a home in Africa for a consciousness formed in and by a language whose history lies on another continent . . . an Africa in the interior of the Africa we seem to see."[4] It is this quality which allows for a reading of Clouts alongside the Afrikaans poets Ingrid Jonker and Adam Small, and the other poets in Section I (all of whom, like Small, wrote from across the divide of colour).

As Coetzee suggests, an "interior Africa" is lodged not only at the heart of Clouts's vision but in his language. At times this is boiled down to a sparse scattering of small tough words, an arid Karoo landscape of the English-speaking mind. Elsewhere, as in the "Hotknife" poems, he takes on, to humorous effect, the Cape Coloured idiom known as "Gammat taal" – the same idiom which weeps and chuckles its way through much of Adam Small's work, infecting even the solemn tones of a pulpit sermon ("Come, Let Us Sing"; "Great Krismis Prayer").

Stretching between the work of these poets, there lies a common landscape, sometimes only tentatively acknowledged, sometimes merely glimpsed from across a wall of difficulty or comfort, yet nonetheless palpable in both physical and human terms. This same landscape is contracted and deadened in the poems by Sob. W. Nkuhlu and St. J. Page Yako; Dennis Brutus is imprisoned in its dark gut, while his onetime high-school student, Arthur Nortje, views it with ultimately fatal longing from out of his exile.

These poets began publishing substantially in the late 1950s and early 1960s. Nineteen sixty was the year of the Sharpeville massacre, of massive protests in Langa township and elsewhere; it was also the year when the African National Congress and the Pan Africanist Congress were banned, when the iron pillow of official apartheid descended with asphyxiating weight on the country.

The result can be strikingly seen in biographies of those poets who established themselves slightly later. Breyten Breytenbach and Mongane Wally Serote spent time in jail as political prisoners; both, along with Wopko Jensma, Njabulo S. Ndebele, Mbuyiseni Oswald Mtshali, Mandla Langa, Mazisi Kunene, Sheila Cussons, and Jeni Couzyn, have lived outside the country, for the most part in forced or voluntary exile. Jensma has been in and out of sheltered homes and psychiatric hospitals; Eva Bezwoda, like Ingrid Jonker and probably Arthur Nortje before her, committed suicide.

Breytenbach speaks of a country "whose cities were linked by arteries . . . to make travel easier between one prison and another."[5] Yet, within this desolation, there was still cause for hope. By the late 1960s, a movement had begun stirring which would give rise to a wave of strikes in Durban; in the townships, news came crackling over transistor radios of the exploits of Frelimo, the guerrilla movement fighting Portuguese occupation just next door in Mozambique. In the early 1970s, the Black Consciousness movement took root, affirming black political and cultural identity in the face of the nationwide drought of white/black relations.

The alchemy of despair and hope is powerfully at work in many of the poems here. Many are jagged, uneasy, deepened with shadow. Yet at the same time they make a particular music, translated from the steel strings of a migrant guitar, the jive of a pennywhistle, the pared-down sorrow of the blues. It is the strength of this music which carries them beyond the wooden words of party politics, the exclamation marks of the sloganeer, to reveal the tangible images and elemental moments of their experience, soaked in the energies of life and death. They dispense with any regular meter or form, breaking through the deliberate, finely controlled, and ultimately defensive gauze of words which characterized the poetry written by whites up to (and even beyond) this period.

White poets like Breytenbach and Jensma jettison the guilt and "polite cowardice"[6] associated with this poetry; black poets, on the other hand, often avoid the belittling stance of the victim. All situate themselves in the thick of the atmosphere they write about – though paradoxically, they may be doing so out of exile. The result, in the work of a poet like Jensma, is the evocation of precisely that frontier-leaping life and hybrid language which apartheid policy aimed to stop in its tracks. Once named "the first wholly integrated South African,"[7] it is a jarring irony that today he should be mentally ill.

Many poems of this period are filled with the strong, refracted light of memory. This is not surprising given the remove – often that of prison or exile – from which they were written. There is paleolithic memory (Wilma Stockenström), ancestral memory (Breytenbach, Kunene), childhood memory (Ndebele, Cussons, Couzyn); the memory of the outside world in Breytenbach's prison poetry; and, by way of contrast, the political amnesia Mtshali refers to in "The Detribalised." Though the theme of memory is as natural to poetry as blood is to the heart, it takes on particular significance in a country where history has become the property of the state, where ancestry is a tool of discrimination, where it took a poet like Serote, in "For Don M. – Banned," to remind his readers that time did not, after all, stand still.

The country at large was shaken into this realization by the 1976 children's revolt in Soweto and elsewhere. There was, however, little depth of time in many of the poems written immediately after this period, particularly those by blacks expressing a self-assertive rage as searing and ephemeral as fire (an image suggested by Oupa Thando Mthimkulu's poem "Nineteen Seventy-Six"). A sense of memory, or wider history, was precluded by the urgency of their political purpose.

A multitude of previously unheard voices detonated into print, notably across the pages of *Staffrider* magazine, but few carried further than the length of a text or two. I have not, for example, been able to discover anything at all about K. Zwide, outside of the oblique and desperate beauty of his or her poem "Wooden Spoon."

There are, however, notable exceptions to this pattern. One is Chris van Wyk with his wry, lucid humour and the sense of play that hones his anger. Another is Mafika Gwala, bending the English language to his own subversive purposes (as Sipho Sepamla does in "Da Same, Da Same"), setting lines of Zulu explosively against it, elbowing through the tight confines of daily life to make way for "the emergence of a new speaking voice."[8]

Also writing during this period were white poets such as Patrick Cullinan, Stephen Gray, Don Maclennan, and Douglas Livingstone, who, with their more inward and at times metaphysical vision, generally situate themselves at a discrete tangent to the wheel of change in society and language. As a result, they are sometimes able to broach subjects inaccessible to their more engaged con- temporaries. Cullinan, in "North," for example, enters the world of a Bushman tribe fleeing destruction in the nineteenth century. At the same time, they occasionally record from a distance the pressures that come steaming through the work of their black contemporaries, as in Gray's poem "Local History." And the description of nature, so often turned into an external, aesthetic event in South African poetry, lends sharpness to more personal preoccupations.

The same might be said of the poems by Stephen Watson and Phil du Plessis. Yet in the landscapes they portray in the 1980s, there is a nascent violence, which is translated into wider social terms by other poets of this period who are (with the exception here of Gcina Mhlophe, Donald Parenzee, and Andries Walter Oliphant) white. The toxic effects of apartheid have now inescapably penetrated the air well beyond the vacuum of the ghettos.

In 1984 the government established a tricameral parliament (for whites, "Coloureds," and Indians), which continued to lock blacks out of their own country. Soon afterwards, opposition forces gathered under the umbrella of the United Democratic Front. There followed years of "unrest," a term applied euphemistically to street warfare, killings, strikes, and mass funerals, which often ended in further bloodshed, none of which was dammed up by two states of emergency. As Jensma, Serote, Breytenbach, and others had done previously, poets here speak of the troubled outer world from within the highly charged field of their own intimate vision: it is inside the heart that bodies lie slaughtered in Robert Berold's "Dark City."

In certain poems the poet's vision stretches out along the axes of time and space. This is the case in the few lines of Parenzee's "The Raining." Jeremy Cronin, in his intimate political praise-poem "Walking on Air," takes in fifty years of South African history. The poem more frequently serves as a place of wide-angle witnessing, the self only one position from which to see.

When Cronin decides "[t]o learn how to speak / With the voices of the land," he cannot be unaware that others, including Clouts, Small, Jensma, and Gwala, have, in different ways, preceded him. But now the land has become a more persistently personal question, though its physical and political dimensions are by no means forgotten. This is the case in Cronin's own poems, for example, in Kelwyn Sole's "The National Question," or Ingrid de Kok's "To Drink Its Water."

At the same time, the worlds of very different people can be rendered, explored, and extended from within the poet's own highly coloured, intimate language, as in Antjie Krog's "lovesong after the music of K. E. Ntsane," Oliphant's "The Hunger Striker," or "Heart's Hunger" by Karen Press.

Several of these poets, like those who began to establish themselves in the 1990s, have published consistently in *New Coin* magazine, edited since 1989 by Robert Berold.[9] Discussing the language of this work, Berold says:

> It feels like an exciting movement is happening in English poetry in this country: the printed poetry of voice. . . . The English language, the language of settlerdom, power and commerce, is being shaped by African sensibilities and forms – African not necessarily meaning black. Increasingly since the 1970s and particularly since the unbanning of the A.N.C. and the demythologization of Mandela, poets are more and more using the living language, breaking the grids of formal political or literary orthodoxy.[10]

"The printed poetry of voice" is a term that can be applied not only to many poems published in the 1980s, but also to those which have appeared since 1990, the year of Nelson Mandela's release and the legalization of opposition parties. South Africa's first democratic elections occured in 1994, followed by the adoption of a new constitution in 1996. The new malleability of social structure and atmosphere is summed up in Tatamkhulu Afrika's image, the "lava of the land" ("The Mugging").[11]

At the same time, new margins of doubt and dissent, articulated previously by Kelwyn Sole, appear here in poems by Afrika, Mxolisi M. Nyezwa, Lesego Rampolokeng, and Seitlhamo Motsapi. The language used by these last two poets, though very different, shares an ebullient, biting quality which emperils both the Queen's English and the fresh, faulty new edifices of South African society. Sole points to a tendency, shared, in my opinion, by an earlier writer such as Gwala, but nonetheless "little apparent among earlier South African poets to whom English is not a first language:

an ability to manipulate, play with, and subvert its forms and expressions from the inside."[12]

In Motsapi's poems, love and blackness appear as touchstones in a place where "the roads / have become hostile" ("sol/o"). It is not far from such roads that Afrika records a lean, closely observed narrative like "The Mugging." In this poem he attains a sense of vulnerability which informs the emotion of his poems and res-onates with the condition of those people in difficulty he so often writes about.

"To be vulnerable is to be fully human. It's the only way you can bleed into other people," says Antjie Krog.[13] This quality infuses Krog's own "transparency of the sole," where it takes on a partic-ular political meaning, as delicate fish-children must adapt, biolog-ically and physically, to a new environment. Here, as in work by younger poets such as Lisa Combrinck, Joan Metelerkamp, and Rustum Kozain, the exploration of extreme, personalized vulnera-bility would seem to correspond to a time when the straightjacket has been removed from South African society, the wind of change stinging against newly exposed skin.

Since 1990, some poets have extended their work over a wider, less directly personal territory. For example, Karen Press, in her poem "Tiresias in the City of Heroes," makes an inventory of recent violence in South Africa, filtering it through a mythological vision. Johann de Lange's incantatory poem "Koos Prinsloo [1957–1994]" moves down the East African Rift Valley in search of the origin of AIDS. In a wide-ranging project of which only small extracts are printed here, Ari Sitas's "Slave Trades" enters nineteenth-century history by the high road of the imagination, giving richly textured voice to both Arthur Rimbaud and the wife he took as a slave trader in Abyssinia.

And Stephen Watson, in the poems which open this anthology, enters the same century by a very different route. These poems are what he himself terms "versions" of /Xam narratives dating back to the 1870s.[14] Each narrative was recounted by one of three people, //Kabbo, Dia!kwain, and /Han≠kasso, all of them convicts, to the German linguist W. H. Bleek and his sister-in-law Lucy Lloyd. A few of the original Bleek texts, reprinted about thirty years ago in the notable *Penguin Book of South African Verse*, were said then to be "arrested out of time."[15] Watson has released their spare magic in contemporary lyrical poetry, allowing something of the spirit of the first peoples in South Africa to surface at a time when the county's history is being reshaped and reevaluated.

It is too soon for most poets to look back at the more immediate past. "There was no worse exile than home," writes Oupa Thando Mthimkulu,[16] but few poets can yet give shape to the memory of apartheid's wreckage. Meanwhile, the momentum of change has slowed, and the future is a riddle rather than a dream. This anthology may give the reader some sense of the many well-tried and restlessly innovative ways in which poets are already setting off across the cooling, hardening lava of the land.

Denis Hirson
Paris, October 1996

Notes

1 A notable exception to this general rule is *The Making of a Servant and Other Poems* (Johannesburg: Ophir/Ravan, 1971), comprising translations of Xhosa poetry by Robert Kavanagh and Z. S. Qangule The poems by Sob W Nkuhle and St J Page Yako are reprinted from this fine, slim volume.

2 I am thinking particularly of translations by Liz Gunner and Mafika Gwala in *Musho! Zulu Popular Praises* (East Lansing. Michigan State University Press, 1991), and Jeff Opland's choice of South African poetry, *Words that Circle Words* (Johannesburg: Ad Donker, 1992).

3. J M Coetzee, *White Writing* (New Haven, Conn.: Yale University Press, 1988), 170.

4 Ibid., 172–73

5 Breyten Breytenbach, "Propos Détenus," afterword to *Feu Froid*, trans. Georges-Marie Lory (Paris: Christian Bourgois, 1983), 126

6 Karen Press, interviewed in *New Coin* 29, no. 1 (1993): 23

7. Sheila Roberts, cited on the back cover of Wopko Jensma's *I Must Show You My Clippings* (Johannesburg: Ravan, 1977) See also Jacques Alvarez-Pereyre's statement. "Before seeing his photograph, one could picture [Jensma] as a Cape Malay, or a Tswana from a township where everyone speaks Afro-American slang, or an Afrikaner who has broken with Afrikanerdom, or an English-speaking South African who has spent his childhood among black people. Yet he is white! [He]   seems to have lived several existences in several communities, and this is something of immense significance in a country so compartmentalized and divided as South Africa" (*The Poetry of Commitment in South Africa* [London: Heinemann, 1984], 109–10).

8 Jeremy Cronin, interviewed by Susan Gardner in *Four South African Poets* (Grahamstown National English Literary Museum, 1986), 26

9. *New Coin*, ISEA, Rhodes University, P.O. Box 94, 6140 Grahamstown, South Africa.

10 Robert Berold, *Comment*, no 10 (Summer 1992) 7–8.

11. See also the references to lava in Peter Horn's "The Eruption of Langa, 30th March 1960," and in Johann de Lange's "Koos Prinsloo [1957–1994]" In very different contexts, Stephen Gray mentions lava ("Song of the Gold Coming In"), while Stephen Watson refers to "volcanic peaks" ("North-West Cape, 1985") and Kelwyn Sole to "the volcano sky" ("Poem from Botswana"). All poems in this anthology

12 Kelwyn Sole, "Bird Hearts Taking Wing Trends in Contemporary South African Poetry Written in English," *World Literature Today* 7, no 1 (Winter 1996): 28

13. Unpublished interview with Denis Hirson, May 1995.

14 See Stephen Watson's introduction to his *Return of the Moon* (Cape Town: Carrefour Press, 1991)

15. *The Penguin Book of South African Verse*, ed. Jack Cope and Uys Krige (London Penguin, 1968), 18.

16 Oupa Thando Mthimkulu, "Out of Africa into Exile," unpublished poem c. 1995

Stephen Watson

SONG OF THE BROKEN STRING

Because
of a people,
because of others,
other people
who came
breaking
the string for me,
the earth
is not earth,
this place is
a place now
changed for me.

Because
the string is that which
has broken for me,
this earth
is no longer
the earth to me,
this place
seems no longer
a place to me.

Because
the string is broken,
the country feels
as if it lay
empty before me,
our country seems
as if it lay
both empty before me,
and dead before me.

3

Because
of this string,
because of a people ⌐
breaking the string, ⌐
this earth, my place
is the place
of something –
a thing broken –
that does not
stop sounding,
breaking within me.

from Dia!kwain

[handwritten annotations: "A people break the string"; "place of broken"; "shattered"; "social unity"; "in revolution"; "renewing Consciousness; breaking the string; que -- repeated can—"]

OUR BLOOD MAKES SMOKE

We would know it by our blood, my father used to say,
our blood starting to mist, our blood making this smoke,
that out there in the mists, very early in the morning,
our camp still lost in sleep, a white commando loomed.

We would know it by our bodies, by a blood within
which trembling, shaking, would start to make the smoke,
a smoke which then would sit before us, burning in our eyes –
it was by blood, by smoking blood, we knew the danger near.

Thus we heard the horses, long before we heard their hooves.
Thus we smelt the gunfire, long before the bullets flew.
A commando was upon us, so our blood's smoke foretold.
We would know it by our blood: that day there would be war.

And we fought back fiercely, through our smoking blood.
We would fight back in the mist, armoured by this blood.
We fought on until we knew, till our blood also knew,
its smoke clearing at last, the white men were beaten back.

4

And we were left there then, with our exhausted blood.
Afterwards we were left there, finding our own bodies,
our blood, used up, exhausted, in foretelling all we'd see:
earth wet with the wounded, our dead lying all around.

But it was by blood Xaa-ttin, my father, used to say,
in blood, our bodies' smoking, we knew what came for us.
Our blood made mist, our blood made smoke, he'd say,
the day of a white commando, each day our end drew near

from Dia!kwain

RAIN IN A DEAD MAN'S FOOTSTEPS

When a person dies
a rain starts falling,
filling, erasing his living footsteps,
filling the hollows
of a dead man's footsteps
so the footsteps themselves
will no longer be there.

When we have put
him into the ground,
put him down into his grave,
the rain comes to wash
his footsteps' hollows;
all trace is erased
of the spoor that we knew.

Even when
we have not yet covered
the grave with cut bushes,
before we have piled
stones on cut bushes

5

(so the bushes themselves
will not lie there naked),

A rain starts falling,
filling his footsteps;
there is rain erasing
the footsteps that were his,
rainwater destroys
that by which he was known,
there is rain
in a dead man's footsteps.

from /Han≠kasso

THE RAIN THAT IS MALE

The rain that is male is an angry rain.
It brings with it lightning loud like our fear.
It brings water storming, making smoke out of dust

And we, we beat our navels with our rigid fists.
We, we press a hand, flat to the navel.
We snap our fingers at the angry, male rain.

And we stand outside in the force of the water,
we stand out in the open, close to its thunder,
we snap our fingers and chant while it falls:

"Rain, be gone quickly! Fall but be gone!
Rain, turn away! Turn back from this place!
Rain, take your anger, be gone from our place!"

For we want the other, the rain that is female,
the one that falls softly, soaking into the ground,
the one we can welcome, feeding the plains –

So bushes sprout green, springbok come galloping

from /Han≠kasso

THE SOUND OF THE STARS

When I slept at my grandfather's, in his hut,
I would sit with him, outside in the cool.
I would ask him about the sound which I heard,
which I sometimes seemed to hear speaking.
He'd say it was stars that were speaking.
"The stars say Tsau! They say Tsau! Tsau!"
They are cursing the springbok's eyes, he'd say.
"This is the sound that stars like to make;
and summer's the time they like to sound."

When at my grandfather's, I listened to stars.
I could hear the sound, the speech of the stars.
Tsatsi would say it was these that I heard,
that they were cursing the springboks' eyes
to help us in hunting, in tracking down game.
Later, when full-grown, and a hunter as well,
I was the one who listened, still listened.
I could sit there and hear it come very close:
the star-sound Tsau, sounding Tsau! Tsau!

from /Han≠kasso

THE SUN, THE MOON AND THE KNIFE

The moon is still full, still alive
as she hangs in the sky just before dawn.

As soon as the sun goes down in the west,
the moon in the east grows ever fuller,

she climbs the sky, her face more burnished,
her belly swelling, full of moon-children,
travelling the sky from one end to the other,
climbing the night from the eastern quarter
till she hangs here, huge, still full, still alive,
shining in the west just as day breaks.

And as soon as the sun comes up in the east,
he reaches far over the length of the earth.
He swiftly pierces the moon's flesh with his knife –
till she who is full, and shining, and alive,
this moon who has speech now has to cry out:
"Sun, leave my children, leave them alone!
Your knife is murdering my unborn moon-children.
The blade of your light stabs our light to death.
Let them still live! Let me, the moon, shine!"

She calls this out while still full in the sky,
still alive in the dawn, before she starts fading.
You can hear her call quickly, hear her cry out
when, each day beginning, the sun lifts up,
takes up his knife to kill her moon-children.
She calls out with a cry, a cry so piercing
that it almost breaks the blade of first light.
Each day she cries out, "Sun, leave my children!
Don't make them die!" And day has broken.

from //Kabbo

THE NATURE OF /KAGGEN

/Kaggen, old trickster, magician, also called Mantis,
maker of the moon, of the eland, and also of trouble,
though you lie in the fire, your flesh now on fire,
though you lie there writhing in the coals' red heat,

your skin blistered, in tatters, your bones blackening fast
(and how you deserved it, you scoundrel, always picking
    a fight!) –

You can still change the world by dreaming the world,
you still have your tricks, old unteachable, untamable;
you could still make an eland from a piece of old shoe,
you could still create the moon from an old, bent shoe;
old incorrigible, magician, old /Kaggen you slyboots,
your Hartebeest children, the quivers for your arrows
could still fly to you, unaided, at no more than a word! –

Even then old trickster, young trickster, even there in that fire,
your arms sprouted feathers, you flew out of the flames;
even then, in that heat, you conjured feathers amidst fire,
you flew out of its blistering to wet your burnt flesh;
O survivor of fire, of hot coals, old rascal even then
you again found the water-pool to wash off your feathers,
you flew free, unlike us, once more cock of the walk,
you flew free, your limbs feathered, a bird's, unlike ours,
you flew off, unlike us, your arms working like wings!

from //Kabbo

FIREBOWL

Kalahari Bushman fires flowing
in the hollows of the desert
click all night
stick stuck upright
click
click
of starlight
bowstring
toes of the eland
thk thk the big raindrops
tk tk tk the sandgrains
drinking.

Sssskla!
sparks of honey
arrowheads
we who dance
around the circle
around the circle
spoor him
find him

my arrow clings to the thick thick
grunt of darkness
my arrow sings through fire

we who dance we find
the
fire
of the fire.

Innie pondok he wait for me
he say you know wy
he say you know wy, Hotknife.

He say
you know wy, Hotknife
you know wy, you Skollie baasted.

So engry, maaster.
No one say dat to me.
Ony my fa'rer say dat to me.

Nellie newwe
tol' me she was married sir
she newwe tol' me she was married sir.

It was luck
but it was bad luck, maaster.

I am Hotknife
of Capricorn
an she was in de Crab sir. It was tiekets.

She newwe tol' me she was married sir.
She was hot for me, hot.
I'm sorrie sir: are you married, maaster?

I'm a man sir
ennytime, bu' dis was ekstra special condieshns

She say Hotknife, swietaat, you a fat man.
Sa! ten years for luff sir.
I'll newwe kiela man again

no, not till I die, maaster
not for a woman, maaster.
She can be so hot for me and I'll not kiela man sir. . . .

STICK SONG

Whittled fine from end to end
driven through and left there
one point prongs the Arctic
one, Antarctic
round it rolls.
Draw out that stick with a swoop of the hand
watch me if you can, I'll do it.
The world's last poem kills it
the seas begin to fly
I write this quickly;
please, boetie
blink your eye.

NORTH WIND

In your long bleak blowing
the berries cluster thick
and green, and plot in several places
in their bush a nest of glowing.

Exploding amongst the leaves
you part the berries.
Parting the berries
you clutch more leaves
and then more berries:
(darker green,
more boisterous fire).

Brunt of tension, wing of night,
beat and beat and beat and blow.
What am I now, sweet berry?
A dragonish manoeuvre tugs and bends,
twigs tangle at the lightning of their ends
The berries ride, I feel the pithy plok.
A secret hits my heart and swings away.
I know that I shall burn at break of day.

WITHIN

You look long about you
intent on the world
on a midsummer day;
the sea flames hard
it is rumpled like tin,
the sun is burning
dimension away.
If you cast a pebble down
it will clatter on the waves,
your eye cannot go in.
And it cannot find a tree
standing generous and full
or a house or flower
with individual power;
and it must not look within,
hardness afflicts you,
flat is the world you'd find:
a row of wooden rooftops
that can easily topple
and bring the heart down
and bring down the mind.

AFTER THE RIOT

We cannot walk tonight. The air is crazy,
like dreams turned loose to make the world their own.
Take down a glass and sip cool calming water.
Through it you'll see how great your thumb has grown

What's closest to us now is best. The door
slams in the wind, so put a wedge to it.
Hands on the bannister seem to feel a trembling
as if the wood held thunder and must split.

Is it by chance your frock is all of faces
that stare at a fateful image in the dark?
Put on your dress of wheels and keep life turning
turning to summer, although we know the spark

has set our lives afire and we are burning.
We swim in waters circled by a shark.
The best is to undress then, very slowly,
and feel your beauty pulsing in the dark.

POETRY IS DEATH CAST OUT

Poetry is death cast out
though it gives one chance to retaliate.
Death takes it but the poem moves
a little further beyond death's gate,

and I know the proof of this. Once walking
amongst bushes and lizard stones I found
a little further than I had thought
to go, a stream with a singing sound.

Ingrid Jonker

"I WENT SEARCHING FOR THE WAY OF MY BODY . . . "

I went searching for the way of my body
and could find only the strange scars in the dust
Tracks of blue wildebeest elephants and leopards
trampled across the safe secret of the white path
Oh I wanted simply to know your shadow, steenbokkie
and the near weightlessness of your fleeing shape

translated from the Afrikaans by Jack Cope

TOKOLOSHE

We children knew it all along
you eat devil's food
we like sugar-root and sundew
but each one as he should

has his own love. In the bush
one plays with water one with clay
till noontide like the redbreast
and the sun round out the day

Then we no longer see your smiles
your laugh of light
we see the dark side of your face
scared of things that catch and bite

Scared of mocking scared to laugh
we scatter from the bush
we children always knew they call
you Love, my tokoloshe

translated from the Afrikaans by Jack Cope

BITTERBERRY DAYBREAK

Bitterberry daybreak
bitterberry sun
a mirror has broken
between me and him.

If I look for the highway
where I can flee
his words make the tracks
twist away from me.

Pinewood of memory
pinewood lost again
if I wander from the highway
I stumble into pain.

Parrot-loud echo
cheating with his fun
till I turn around deceived
to see the teaser run.

Echo is no answer
he answers everyone
bitterberry daybreak
bitterberry sun.

translated from the Afrikaans by Cherry Clayton

PREGNANT WOMAN

I lie under the crust of the night singing,
curled up in the sewer, singing,
and my bloodchild lies in the water.

16

I play that I'm a child:
gooseberries, gooseberries and heather
kukumakrankas and anise
and the tadpole glides
in the slime of the stream
in my body
my foam-white reflection;
but sewer oh sewer,
my bloodchild lies in the water.

Still singing fleshrose our bloodsong
I and my yesterday,
my yesterday hangs under my heart
my red gladiolus my cradling world
and my heart that sings like a cicada,
my cicada-heart sings like a cicada;
but sewer oh sewer,
my bloodchild lies in the water.

I play that I'm happy:
look where the firefly sparkles!
the moon-disc, a wet snout that quivers –
but with the morning, the limping midwife,
grey and shivering on the sliding hills,
I push you out through the crust into daylight,
oh sorrowing owl, great owl of the daylight,
free from my womb but besmeared,
with my tears all smeared
and tainted with sadness.

Sewer oh sewer
I lie trembling, singing
how else but trembling
with my bloodchild under your water . . . ?

translated from the Afrikaans by Jack Cope

She shelters me in the profusion of her lap
She says my throat is not going to be cut
She says I'm not being put under house-arrest
She says I'm not dying of the galloping consumption of love
She doesn't know I am hungry
She doesn't know I am afraid
She doesn't know cockcrow and house-arrest are a pair
She is my mother
With cups of tea she paralyses Table Mountain
and her hands are as cool as spoons

translated from the Afrikaans by Jack Cope

THE CHILD WHO WAS SHOT DEAD BY SOLDIERS

IN NYANGA

The child is not dead
the child lifts his fists against his mother
who screams Afrika shouts the scent
of freedom and the veld
in the locations of the cordoned heart

The child lifts his fists against his father
in the march of the generations
who are shouting Afrika shout the scent
of righteousness and blood
in the streets of his warrior pride

The child is not dead
not at Langa not at Nyanga
not at Orlando not at Sharpeville
not at the police station in Philippi
where he lies with a bullet through his brain

Spectre of the

The child is the shadow of the soldiers *(haunting")*
on guard with rifles saracens and batons
the child is present at all gatherings and law-giving
the child peers through house windows and into the hearts
   of mothers ⇒ *Laws of Daughters*
the child who wanted just to play in the sun at Nyanga is
   everywhere
the child grown to a man treks all over Africa
the child grown to a giant travels through the whole world

Without a pass

translated from the Afrikaans by Jack Cope and William Plomer

THE LAND OF THE PEOPLE ONCE LIVING

Ask me the news from home and I will tell you.
Ask me about dreams and I will reveal their meaning.
I dreamt I rode a white horse,
Long like the green tree snake itself.
A thing that swam in air while the breeze murmured.
My heart was happy and reared high with joy.
I ought to have asked questions but I didn't,
Because of the magic of the people once living.
I was afraid lest I should end up hanging
Between those two sharp horns
But the fear and the shame passed –
Because I am going to the land of the people once living.

Fascinating land, magnetic, magical,
Land of wealth and flowers, land of plenty,
Glamorous, fat, endowed.
We see it in our minds, our hearts,
Our brains, our spirits.
I sing the land of the people once living,
        the land of our great ancestors.
I sing the land of heroes and the time-honoured.

Hail, you wizards, hail, you fashioners
And diviners, wizards of the river-frogs,
I say to you sages and rainmakers,
You have done well, you have perfected the knowledge of roots
You saw proportion, fortune, magic and strength
In those of the boer-boon tree and the sacred tambuti,
In the bark of the kakoedoorn tree and the corkwood.
You work magic where the wild garlic grows.
How can I know one root from another?
Or the secret knowledge of the great river?
For your magic begins with visions
And then sinks out of sight in the waters of the great river.

Yonder are the councils, seated on their thrones,
In the land of the people once living and those long since dead.
We do not refer to the heroes, the time-honoured,
Because even here they have authority.
He who wears the plume in this world
Will wear it in the next – a man.
There are others who sit around, lounging about – they are chaff,
Of no importance, without a name, no dignity.

Nowadays, I say, traditional enmities,
It appears, have disappeared.
The snake and the frog eat together.
The rope on the milking can has come adrift.
The condition of the air is stench,
The jackal feeds with the lamb,
The elephant waits on the ant.
We live in a land which unsettles the heart
For even when we are happy, we remain ill at ease,
Even when we have heard the reasons, we feel wronged.
Although we've understanding, we do not understand,
Even though we're satisfied, we behave riotously.
The heart is restless, tossed from side to side,
As if it would burst out, roots and all.

Heavy-horned cattle fill the kraals,
Black and white cows, cows with young calves,
Milking cows, red ones, chocolate, grey,
Oxen with a white blaze on the forehead,
Raising the dust, goring, bellowing,
Bulls of all different colours like leopards,
Spoiling for a fight, lowering at each other.

Fields and scrub are white and grey
With sheep and goats of all colours.
It rolls away before the eye like the sea,
One minute it's here, the next it's there.

Grass whose greenness makes you tremble with awe,
The mouth waters to look at it.
The rustling breezes brush against it,
Not cold, not hot – cool, as it should be.

Alas, ideal land, lukewarm people,
We feel for you, we cry out for you.
Mercy, you honoured men of royal descent.
Mercy, for see how the marrows cover the land,
Look, even the segments are sprouting –
Corn has always been the food of men.
We do not eat it in this mortal world alone
But we eat it and bear it away as food for our journey.
We swallow a mouthful in this world and a mouthful in the next.

Look at the defiling snake entering the house,
Though it seems that even children fondle it these days.
The old men bind it about the waist like a belt –
I said nowadays all enmity has disappeared.
Where is your sting, viper?
Where is your cunning, poisonous lizard?
Where is your trickery, ringhals?

They dance, prance, shake, shiver,
Sing, imagine, marry, initiate,
They feast, eat their fill where there's no haggling,
The children walk with full bellies, waddling from side to side,
Full of sourmilk, full of milk sucked straight from the udder.
No one drinks or makes love out of place,
No rioting, no turmoil.
All these were cast into oblivion and the end of all.

Oh the beauty, the majesty of the people once living
Feeds the spirit, nurses it.
The spirit is ripe and full and at rest.
Blissful with sleeping it stays,

Where only beautiful thoughts and memories
Dance before the eye of the soul.
It is a land of green spring,
The land Mhlakaza's daughter spoke about.
Awu, land of the people once living and those long dead,
Land where the soul may rest and breathe at peace.
It is a land of truth, as there is no punishment.
A land with no tears, as no one is troubled.
This is no living land, only the future can bring us one.

translated from the Xhosa by Robert Kavanagh and Z. S. Qangule

St. J. Page Yako

THE CONTRACTION AND ENCLOSURE OF THE LAND

Thus spake the heirs of the land
Although it is no longer ours.
This land will be folded like a blanket
Till it is like the palm of a hand.
The racing ox will become entangled in the wire,
Too weak to dance free, it will be worn
Out by the dance of the yoke and the plough.
They will crowd us together like tadpoles
In a calabash ladle. Our girls
Will have their lobola paid with paper,
Coins that come and go, come and go.
Blood should not be spilled, so they say
Nowadays, to unite the different peoples,
Until we no longer care for each other,
As a cow licks her calf, when love
And nature urge her to do so.
Can money bring people together?
Yes, a man may have words with his son's wife,
His son need no longer respect her mother.

Yes, we fold up our knees,
It's impossible to stretch out,
Because the land has been hedged in.

translated from the Xhosa by Robert Kavanagh and Z. S. Qangule

Dennis Brutus

NIGHTSONG: CITY

Sleep well, my love, sleep well:
the harbour lights glaze over restless docks,
police cars cockroach through the tunnel streets;

from the shanties creaking iron-sheets
violence like a bug-infested rag is tossed
and fear is immanent as sound in the wind-swung bell;

the long day's anger pants from sand and rocks;
but for this breathing night at least,
my land, my love, sleep well.

COLD

the clammy cement
sucks our naked feet

a rheumy yellow bulb
lights a damp grey wall

the stubbled grass
wet with three o'clock dew
is black with glittery edges;

we sit on the concrete,
stuff with our fingers
the sugarless pap
into our mouths

then labour erect;

form lines;

steel ourselves into fortitude
or accept an image of ourselves
numb with resigned acceptance;

the grizzled senior warder comments:
"Things like these
I have no time for;
they are worse than rats;
you can only shoot them."

Overhead
the large frosty glitter of the stars
the Southern Cross flowering low;

the chains on our ankles
and wrists
that pair us together
jangle

glitter.

We begin to move
    awkwardly.

[Colesberg: en route to Robben Island]

WAITING

The isolation of exile is a gutted
warehouse at the back of pleasure streets:
the waterfront of limbo stretches panoramically –
night the beautifier lets the lights
dance across the wharf.
I peer through the skull's black windows
wondering what can credibly save me.
The poem trails across the ruined wall
a solitary snail, or phosphorescently
swims into vision like a fish
through a hole in the mind's foundation, acute
as a glittering nerve.

Origins trouble the voyager much, those roots
that have sipped the waters of another continent.
Africa is gigantic, one cannot begin
to know even the strange behaviour furthest
south in my xenophobic department.
Come back, come back mayibuye
cried the breakers of stone and cried the crowds
cried Mr Kumalo before the withering fire
mayibuye Afrika

Now there is the loneliness of lost
beauties at Cabo de Esperancia, Table Mountain:
all the dead poets who sang of spring's
miraculous recrudescence in the sandscapes of Karoo
sang of thoughts that pierced like arrows, spoke
through the strangled throat of multi-humanity
bruised like a python in the maggot-fattening sun.

You with your face of pain, your touch of gaiety,
with eyes that could distil me any instant
have passed into some diary, some dead journal

now that the computer, the mechanical notion
obliterates sincerities.
The amplitude of sentiment has brought me no nearer
to anything affectionate,
new magnitude of thought has but betrayed
the lustre of your eyes.

You yourself have vacated the violent arena
for a northern life of semi-snow
under the Distant Early Warning System:
I suffer the radiation burns of silence.
It is not cosmic immensity or catastrophe
that terrifies me:
it is solitude that mutilates,
the night bulb that reveals ash on my sleeve.

Adam Small

Friends,
let us open up the Good Book
and read from it –
o Mos Holy Spirit
let these words go right t our heart –
from the secon book a Mosas
from Ex'dus,
fourth chapter, firs an secon verse –
o God
make for us with these words a light as that of candles! –

an Mosas answered an he said: but what
if they don b'lieve me, don take up my words
if they say the Lord didn't never appear t me at all?

but the Lord said: you shall lead your people
What is in your hand?
an Mosas said: a rod.

Now friends
twas all he had
this man o God
a rod
a great dead stick
an on top of that he was also a stamm'rer

but the Lord spoke with him at length
how with that stick he had stricken dead
the Egyptian
an Mosas let his great big head hang down
an
an sunly that selfsame rod was become a serpent!

now friends
even unto me has the Lord brought

his wonderworks
he has asked me what is in my hand
an friends
in my hand is my guitar

come, let us sing

translated from the Afrikaans by Mike Dickman

FROM GREAT KRISMIS PRAYER

Lord
once again we praise you
you what came f' the redemption of the worl
you what was born so many Krismises ago
in Bethlehem

ja in Bethlehem Lord
in the stable
by the donkey
by the cow
in the crib
on the earth floor
on the floor of sand Lord
in a place that stank
in a place where a person got sick from the stink

we know such places Lord
ja we know them
we got duplicates of them allover
in Windemere
in Distrik Six
in Blouvlei here jis otherside Wynberg by Retreat

an that's why we praise you again this Krismis Lord
jis you

jis you who's got the biggest esperience of us all
of this kind of places
only you can help us

only you can perhaps again
this Krismis Lord let
a new Mosas be born for us here

a new Mosas
a new Mosas
o Lord, our Mosas –
we'll hide him away Lord, we got lotsa hidingplaces
from the daggers what don' like him –
to lead us, the whole bunch of us
lead us to the plain before the vineyards of Canaan
of Canaan Lord
Lord, our Canaan

translated from the Afrikaans by Mike Dickman

PREACHER

you a Prophet a Jesus?
a prophet?
you wit yo palace-house?
you wit yo airmobile?
you wit that kinda sad smile a yours?
an yo tears
an yo huffanpuff up onna pulpit
an yo plate piled high wit braaivleis pertaties an meat?

yo house the desert? boy! folks is really gonna think you summin!
an how ja like yo bare lil feet f' that streamline thing
how ja like yo camelskin toga
how ja like ya plateful locust an wile honey?

translated from the Afrikaans by Mike Dickman

Please mad'm
c'mon smile
jis look
our little old tents is piled high wit joy

how can mad'm look so sour
shame on you shame
d'you think life's vinegar
an where's mad'm buyin it then
cause i bet it's real expensive

nah, mad'm
c'mon, c'mon smile
look over there
our little old tents is piled high wit joy

This white dame can't laugh
jis gives orders:
there's nuthin I want,
the coon formal as hell

But mad'm, pawpaw, pawpaw an banana
an juicy grapes out the heart of Canaan
or maybe the lady would fancy a fig
jis look how swollen it is
plumped right out from top to bottom
don' blush now mad'm
we got the leaf right here
ja well maybe

I don' want nuthin hear!

But mad'm

I don' want nuthin do you hear!

32

But mad'm

You, you coolie
I'm going to call the cops!

The fruitboy's voice suddenly muffled
cops, cops?
hey c'mon lady, don' be so mean
jis say g'bye nicely
hey guess what
them bare-arse ole nec'trines still blowin mad'm a kissie goodbye

The white woman stomps off
across the parade,
clippety-clop, clippety-clop

Hey lady, hey
mad'm sho she don wanna try our guavas
guarantee 'm lady
great f' the nerves!

translated from the Afrikaans by Mike Dickman

GESONDHEID!

Old slave tree
memories of
great grandfather
you bring me

and great grandmother's
in the row
of those here honoured
by Monument for Huguenot

one from primal Malabar
one from clearest France
and they came entirely
under the star
of Chance

o Land of Sunshine
my honour you trample down
but in your blessed wine
am I and my brown
o taste whene'er you toast
to God knows what
and I am very sad
great grandmother's clarity
great grandfather's sweat!

FIVE QUATRAINS FROM BLACK BRONZE

BEAUTIFUL

My nipples are the noses, wet like dew
of early morning or late night
of two black lambs – two playful karakul:
their supple darkness makes your manhood new

●

Kiss, kiss this purple pulse, my mouth
this joyous and warm wound filled full with blood
this crimson throbbing bird of song
that will in winter sing you to the Summer South

●

Pluck at my pomegranate breasts and throw each purple pip
back of your open throat; don't fear the full feast
on this seed so rich: for in this joy of flesh
is blended pain also – the slave-chain and the whip

●

Their vineyard's keeper thought they I would be,
harvesting their grapes: their wood to hew
But the Sun, intoxicating, would not let me be
Would not let me break my dark beauty

●

Thrust in your hand, deep in, and take and eat
from this, my body's basket – a latticed bamboo basket
filled with bread, black bread baked in the earth
brown crusted bread to eat with sweet palm wine and meat

Mongane Wally Serote

ALEXANDRA

Were it possible to say,
Mother, I have seen more beautiful mothers,
A most loving mother,
And tell her there I will go,
Alexandra, I would have long gone from you.

But we have only one mother, none can replace,
Just as we have no choice to be born,
We can't choose mothers;
We fall out of them like we fall out of life to death.

And Alexandra,
My beginning was knotted to you,
Just like you knot my destiny.
You throb in my inside silences
You are silent in my heart-beat that's loud to me.
Alexandra often I've cried.
When I was thirsty my tongue tasted dust,
Dust burdening your nipples.
I cry Alexandra when I am thirsty.
Your breasts ooze the dirty waters of your dongas,
Waters diluted with the blood of my brothers, your children,
Who once chose dongas for death-beds.
Do you love me Alexandra, or what are you doing to me?

You frighten me, Mama,
You wear expressions like you would be nasty to me,
You frighten me, Mama,
When I lie on your breast to rest, something tells me,
You are bloody cruel.
Alexandra, hell
What have you done to me?
I have seen people but I feel like I'm not one,
Alexandra what are you doing to me?

39

I feel I have sunk to such meekness!
I lie flat while others walk on me to far places.
I have gone from you, many times,
I come back. [RETURN]
Alexandra, I love you;
I know
When all these worlds became funny to me,
I silently waded back to you
And amid the rubble I lay,
Simple and black.

CITY JOHANNESBURG

This way I salute you:
My hand pulses to my back trousers pocket
Or into my inner jacket pocket
For my pass, my life,
Jo'burg City.
My hand like a starved snake rears my pockets
For my thin, ever lean wallet,
While my stomach groans a friendly smile to hunger,
Jo'burg City.
My stomach also devours coppers and papers
Don't you know?
Jo'burg City, I salute you;
When I run out, or roar in a bus to you,
I leave behind me, my love,
My comic houses and people, my dongas and my ever
    whirling dust,
My death
That's so related to me as a wink to the eye.
Jo'burg City
I travel on your black and white and roboted roads
Through your thick iron breath that you inhale

[At six in the morning and exhale from five noon.]
Jo'burg City
That is the time when I come to you,
When your neon flowers flaunt from your electrical wind,
That is the time when I leave you,
When your neon flowers flaunt their way through the falling
    darkness
On your [cement trees.]
And as I go back, to my love,
My dongas, my dust, my people, my death,
Where death lurks in the dark like a blade in the flesh,
I can feel your roots, anchoring your might, my feebleness
In my flesh, in my mind, in my blood,
And everything about you says it,
That, that is all you need of me.
Jo'burg City, Johannesburg,
Listen when I tell you,
There is no fun, nothing, in it,
When you leave the women and men with such frozen
    expressions,
Expressions that have tears like furrows of soil erosion,
Jo'burg City, you are dry like death,
Jo'burg City, Johannesburg, Jo'burg City.

I WILL WAIT

I have tasted, ever so often,
Hunger like sand on my tongue
And tears like flames have licked my eye-lids
Blurring that which I want to see,
I want to know.
But Oh! often, now and then, everywhere where I have been,
Joy, as real as paths,
Has spread within me like pleasant scenery,

Has run beneath my flesh like rivers glitteringly silver,
And now I know:
Having been so flooded and so dry,
I wait.

OFAY-WATCHER LOOKS BACK

I want to look at what happened;
That done,
As silent as the roots of plants pierce the soil
I look at what happened,
Whether above the houses there is always either smoke or dust,
As there are always flies above a dead dog.
I want to look at what happened.
That done,
As silent as plants show colour: green,
I look at what happened,
When houses make me ask: do people live there?
As there is something wrong when I ask – is that man alive?
I want to look at what happened,
That done,
As silent as the life of a plant that makes you see it
I look at what happened
When knives creep in and out of people
As day and night into time.
I want to look at what happened,
That done,
As silent as plants bloom and the eye tells you:
                         something has happened.
I look at what happened
When jails are becoming necessary homes for people
Like death comes out of disease,

I want to look at what happened.

FOR DON M. – BANNED

it is a dry white season
dark leaves don't last, their brief lives dry out
and with a broken heart they dive down gently headed for
   the earth,
not even bleeding.
it is a dry white season brother,
only the trees know the pain as they still stand erect
dry like steel, their branches dry like wire,
indeed, it is a dry white season
but seasons come to pass.

MILK AND CORN

If my mother's milk was wise enough
as wise as the corn of the field
I would not be here;
Corn comes once in a year, fears other seasons
but not my mother's milk
It gave me life after that big cry
it taught me to suck
to walk
to love
and today I am a man
huge
blackman with experience,
expected to work,
I toil today where the corn refuses to grow
the sweat of my brow drips
splashes on iron-hard rocks under the whipping sun,
but I keep on, I want corn
for I can make milk in some woman
for somebody to suck.

43

I do not know where I have been,
But Brother,
I know I'm coming.
I do not know where I have been,
But Brother,
I know I heard the call.
Hell! where I was I cried silently
Yet I sat there until now.
I do not know where I have been,
But Brother,
I know I'm coming:
I come like a tide of water now,
But Oh! There's sand beneath me!
I do not know where I have been
To feel so weak, Heavens! so weary.
But Brother,
Was that Mankunku's horn?
Hell! my soul aches like a body that has been beaten,
Yet I endured till now.
I do not know where I have been,
But Brother,
I know I'm coming.
I do not know where I have been,
But Brother I come like a storm over the veld,
And Oh! there are stone walls before me!
I do not know where I have been
To have fear so strong like the whirlwind (will it be that brief?)
But Brother,
I know I'm coming.
I do not know where I have been,
But Brother,
Was that Dumile's figure?
Hell, my mind throbs like a heart beat, there's no peace;
And my body of wounds – when will they be scars? –

Yet I can still walk and work and still smile.
I do not know where I have been
But Brother,
I know I'm coming.
I do not know where I have been,
But Brother,
I have a voice like the lightning-thunder over the mountains.
But Oh! there are copper lightning conductors for me!
I do not know where I have been
To have despair so deep and deep and deep
But Brother,
I know I'm coming.
I do not know where I have been
But Brother,
Was that Thoko's voice?
Hell, well, Heavens!

T W O   E X T R A C T S   F R O M   N O   B A B Y   M U S T   W E E P

who am i
lost like this
broken like this
weary like this
who am i
let me touch with my fingers
i have cut my nails,
i hope that my fingers are soft,
as soft as a baby's heel
so i can grope
this thicket dark of what remains after tongues have wagged
and only the stars, the sky, the moon, the mountains and the
    wind
in their silence as they witness
have understood for what it is what had happened,

i hope my nails are cut,
i dip my strength into the depths of the bottom of my love
and like a bird swallowing water its eyes to the sky
i reach out
to touch, to feel the human profile
that half-face
one-eye
half-nose
half-mouth
silent and loaded with sadness
a frail frame sagging beneath that brief moment
between birth and death;
i hope my nails are cut –
boy
what happened
that now you depart having shattered our hearts to bits
having torn our hopes to shreds
leaving behind you
dry cheeks and eyes which have lost the cue to innocence;
we will have to do, gently, gently with the calmness of a cat
that eats its kittens, a ritual –
pick up with our bare hands, your arms which were torn off
your body
put them together
put them in their shattered sockets
and with our bare fingers, nails cut, pick the pieces
of your face which we can find,
and with clean hands, palms and all
gather together your bowels,
wrap them
put them back into the hole where they were when you were
    born
we shall stand back and take the last look at the work
of our hearts
satisfied
we shall seal the coffin and put it into the hole

rest in pieces you beastly corpse – tiro
only the stars, the sky, the moon, the mountains and the wind
will welcome you to their ranks,
we shall lick our paws now and wash our faces
we glad
mothers on this side of the world don't weep no more

●

i turn to you my mother whose warmth i felt with my
unripe flesh
hold my hand, your son is a man
i
i can eat i can laugh
my loins now and then are trapped in flames
my fingers can make life
though i be so wound-riddled, weary
i stride the earth with the rhythm of my wounds
i race this earth
fuelled by the fury of love and hate
i turn to you my mother
you have a warrior in your house
this
i
who've held your nipples between my lips and within my
tongue
i arrive while the earth is asleep
come my mother, hold my hand
black mother let me hold your hand and walk with you
let me feel the odour of your sweat as it falls from
your body
and mirages into the air
let the warmth and sweat of your hand
soak into mine
your hands
these hands which have been wrecked by their toil

they have held my hand in that moment when i laboured to learn
to open my eye
may i hold your hand now
my eye is open and my mind is sweating
i come back to you to hold your hand and let's walk this
earth
let my heart drink from your eyes
that glimmer of love which shone when everything about
you was shaken
hold my hand
let your bosom whisper things to my mind
the songs of this time, this moment, will drink from my soul
but i have been a lost child
named after all the curses of this world
i have been shooed out
i have been trapped, locked tight in the fury of man

my knees show the bone, my palms are worn out
my heart is filled with the sand of the wilderness

"I WILL DIE AND GO TO MY FATHER

I will die and go to my father
in Wellington on long legs
dazzling in the light
where the rooms are heavy and dark
where stars sit like seagulls on the rooftop
and angels dig for worms in the garden,
I will die, pack up a toothbrush,
        take the road
across the Wellington mountains
through the trees and the twilight
and go to my father;

the sun will pound into the earth
the joints will creak with waves of wind
we'll hear the lodgers
scraping around overhead
and play draughts on the back porch
– my old man is such a cheat –
and listen to night's news
on the radio

friends, fellow mortals,
don't tremble; life still hangs
like flesh from our bodies
but death has no shame –
we come and we go
like water from a tap
like sounds from the mouth
like our comings and goings:
it's our bones which will know freedom
        come with me
bound in my death, to my father
in Wellington where the angels
use worms to fish fat stars from heaven;

let us die and decompose and be merry:
my father has a large boarding-house

translated from the Afrikaans by Denis Hirson

MY HERITAGE

"your grandpa"
says my father resting
before the light at the window
his head a dark songbird snared
in the oversized collar
"your grandpa was a farmer

"not all that – er – successful
since he went ploughing and planting
in never-never land and was hardly – er –
dexterous with his hands
but *peu importe*

"in the old days night fell anyway
before anyone could choose his way

"his farm ran down the Fish River
(ah I see again the banks buttocking
steep and lush and blue before me)
but he was a profoundly god-carrying man
a Buddhist – er – or of some other
obscure creed

"Sundays his house teemed black with prayer-people

"with his hands deep in the good clods
your grandpa
died of poverty

but *this* – er – and *this*
he left to you:"

with his voice my father reaches for
and caresses the heavenly spheres
and the sun a hill on fire
mountains with their rumpled cheeks clean acres
flowers humankind even canes wound
with snakes

: *"all this priceless dictionary!"*

translated from the Afrikaans by the poet

"HOW DROWSY WE WERE WRAPPED IN

COOLNESS . . . "

how drowsy we were wrapped in coolness on the floor
the smell of turpentine and fire
the canvas white to our empty eyes
the indifference of the night
and the moon a smile somewhere outside
out of sight
days fall apart like seasons at the panes
a cloud, a face, leaves of rain, this poem,
I want to leave my print on you
I want to brand you with the fire
of solitude
no song of fire as beautiful
as the silver ash of your movements
and your sad body
I wished to draw that sadness from you
and have your body break open
like a city opening
onto a bright landscape

filled with pigeons and the fire of trees
and silver crows out of sight in the night
and the moon a mouth that one can ignite
and then I wished you could have laughed
and your bitter body
my hands of porcelain on your hips
your breath such a dark ache
a sword at my ear
how often were we here
where only silver shadows are left stirring
alone through you I must refuse myself
through you alone I realize I have no harbour
in a burning sea

translated from the Afrikaans by Denis Hirson

THE TRUTH

geynest under gore,
herkne to my roun –

do you still remember when we were dogs
how we used to trot
on little pawed sores
through the tunnels and sluices of the town
streets of flapping yellow sheets
across cobblestones mud dykes loose planks
and leafy avenues
canals which even the rats never explored
do you remember how low we were against the ground
and how exhausted we grew
with flabby bloodlimp rags for tongues
from panting hard up the hill
right through hedges glass walls concrete shafts
past fearsome knots of streets with their spurting traffic lights
foundations drains cellars and cesspools where the heel-

jerks of the hung dead still adorned the breeze
with day and night but a drooping of the eye

till we arrived at the house of old Master R
where we could eat and smoke and drink
vodka for me and tchai for you
and sugary cookies for us both

and our grasp of the city
no one else could know
that it was in reality
a rhythmic intertwining flow

do you still remember when we were dogs
you and I, best beloved?

translated from the Afrikaans by the poet

PLAGIARISM

a man made himself a poem
for his birthday the sixteenth of the ninth –
o, no fancy affair with room and rhyme
and rhythm and iambs and stuff, a rustling tone
bone to pick or other poetic knicknacks –
not under such meagre circumstances as now,
mountain-drawing-your-eyes, steady hours, tree-with-stars,
wife and sea gone – almost
all elements sadly lacking;
still, there were certainly odds and sods around –
he scraped and scrounged, aped what he found
and tried to turn the leftovers
into something with his breath –
even in the desert the tongue has its shade:

first then the man himself, hump on his shoulders –

old numbskull, bumptious baboon,
(but ruin already alive in his seed – that's part of Death's art)
and then the fine hairs on his hands, and the fly
(rechristened Stalin) since it really is a cloud
in the be-all of a cell, and some further words thrown in for
    free –
the sixteenth of the ninth brought him
to sinews and blessings, ten against one, pins and puns –
and running out he had to bring his pants
into the poem – the short khaki ones
worn away by so many, stitched up with purple cotton
here at the waisted parts like an appendix scar
the stigma partly grown into the skin, and the spoon
with 'maximum' stamped (chewed?) into the handle wrought
of unblemished steel, to help him get to the end of the line
("I am defiled! defiled!")
(with a dying flourish he spooned out the thought)
and then there was the ant dragging its body-one-leg-broken
which strayed in from who-knows-where,
and like punctuation when sense is absent
the memory-of-love

having used up everything to hand
he wrapped it circumspectly in fresh paper
meaning to write it out neatly later that evening
but when around nightfall he unfolded the present
the damned paper had already gobbled up the poem;
and the man gripped his hump and humphed a groan:
"my poem, my poem – now what will I have to show for my
birthday the sixteenth of the ninth!"

(made in – or out of? – the Otherplace)

translated from the Afrikaans by Denis Hirson

your letter is delightful, larger and lighter
that the thought of a flower when the dream
is a garden,
                as your letter opens
there is an unfolding of sky, word from outside,
wide spaces,

I slept in green pastures
I lay on the ridge of the valley of the shadow of death
during the last watch of the night
listening to those condemned to die
being led through tunnels in the earth,
                              how they sing
with the breath at their lips
as residents at the point of leaving
a city in flames, how they sing
their breaths like shackles,
                      how they sing
they who are about to jump from light into darkness
they who will be posted to no destination,
terror fills me at the desecration,

the table before me in the presence of my enemies
is bare, I have ash on my head,
my cup is empty,

and I fled to your letter to read
of the orange tree decked out in white blossoms
opening with the sun,
I could smell it on the balcony,
                          I can smell you
lovelier and lighter than the thought of a flower
in this dismal night,

I will be suspended from the sky of your words,
give that I may dwell in your letter
all the days of my life,

envoi,
your letter is wonderful, larger and lighter
than the thought of a flower when the dream
is the earth of a garden,
                              as your letter opens
there is an unfolding of sky, word from outside,
memory,

translated from the Afrikaans by the poet

DECEMBER

following rhythm and road of a poem by Gary Snyder

Six a.m. – jingle
        of night commander
        speeding closer; keys crack
        down the corridor:
out there birds arbour tinkling
tiny bells: in the minute
meshed yard pansies fold open
like moths flagging down the day;
stretch the pallet with bedding on bunk;
in the section bath and shave.
        N— the cleaner, silent, pimpled
        white prison feet,
        brings the porridge, "coffee," bread
        (who's trying to sell me short?)

Voice of section head: Jump to it!
Jump to it! Clean up! Move arse!

Inspection. Cement floor shimmering
a shaven face.

Out for exercise round
    and round the sightless pansies.
    Boer's cap-badge, whiskers, gleam.
    Cut the pocketchief
    lawn short
    and scour slop-bucket white:
    wind weeping in some
    wireless tree.

Ten-thirty lunch: boiled mealies,
beet, maybe meat. Dixies out!
Rinse off and wedge spoon in door.
Eleven o'clock the cell's locked:
                        midday snooze
    draw deep at the fag
    and listen to the Philistines rag.

Two o'clock. Taxi-pads across the floor
once more, Brasso on copper; Ghostkeeper's
    chill eye ringed by the judas;
    try making contact
    with connection.
    Cell ransacked – someone
    must have quacked.
    Stretch the pallet with bedding on bunk.

Three-thirty, graze – soup, "coffee,"
    yellow eye of butter
    framed by bread.
    Dixies out! Buck up!
Rinse off and spoon in door,
both shoes lined up
without feet on corridor floor.

Four o'clock the cell is locked:
Get up! Stand to!
Gaol-bird countdown all motherfuckers you!

Lights on. Dusk
might be falling outside like prayer. Manna.
Listen how being locked up grinds.
                                        Talk to self.

Condemns sing. Outside birds
mirror the tilted
tiny bell sounds; in the tight
meshed yard pansies fold together
like flags wording moths in the night.

Eight o'clock, slumbertime, lights out
            and fire of yearning.
Limelight and torch-blur on catwalk,
rifle-butts thud.
                    Heart burns: sweet
                    smoke in nostrils,
                    thoughts scuffle:
A mugu sobs and bleats in the bush of sleep.

Zazen. Steel and concrete folds
where stars quiver;
            the guard's beat is god
            in the head –
            but stillness in the crop
            breath's penitential exercise.

Sit till midnight. Silently
            invoke this day's negative.
            Bow deep to the wall
            and stretch the pallet out on bunk.
            Stiff under sheets:
            white.

Jingle
of night commander
speeding closer

translated from the Afrikaans by the poet

FOR FRANCOOI VILJOEN

there are things one never forgets oh dissemblers –
cat's paws of darkness over closed eyelids
the brief clear gaping of the bullet's cough
car headlamps slitting the night to ribbons
painted white masks of the buffoon and the whore
the hangman's laughter like a dose of strychnine
the flesh-coloured flame
                              that cannot scorch the satin purse
black rooks on red haystacks
a dwarf with a whistle on the elephant's back
the tower filled for years with whispering fire
the green swollen booming of the sea
the long broken downhill shuffle of old age
braking till it's worn to the knees –
these, the inalienable souvenirs
the heart's tiny mirrors lugged the length of the journey

we all walk that road
of life on its way to death –
murderers, burglars, drug addicts and firebugs
thugs, embezzlers, rapists
and fellow terrorists –
you like I tattooed in lineament and skin
single in our destiny –
till we climb through the gap
into the kitchen pantry
and the earth munches us to the bone
– "finished; dispatched; cracked; home" –

59

go well friends by the light of the body
go well marked by what's never forgotten
to the final prison where all memory goes dark –
hamba kahle!

translated from the Afrikaans by the poet

SPANNER IN THE WHAT? WORKS

i was born 26 july 1939 in ventersdorp
i found myself in a situation

i was born 26 july 1939 in sophiatown
i found myself in a situation

i was born 26 july 1939 in district six
i found myself in a situation

i was born 26 july 1939 in welkom
i found myself in a situation

now, when my mind started to tick
i noticed other humans like me
shaped like me: ears eyes
hair legs arms etc . . . (i checked)
we all cast in the same shackles:
flesh mind feeling smell sight etc . . .

date today is 5 april 1975 i live
at 23 mountain drive derdepoort
phone number: 821-646, post box 26285
i still find myself in a situation

i possess a typewriter and paper
i possess tools to profess i am artist
i possess books, clothes to dress
my flesh; my fingerprint of identity
i do not possess this land, a car
much cash or other valuables

I brought three kids into this world
(as far as i know)
i prefer a private to a public life

(i feel allowed to say)
i suffer from schizophrenia
(they tell me)
i'll die, i suppose, of lung cancer
(if i read the ads correctly)

i hope to live to the age of sixty
i hope to leave some evidence
that i inhabited this world
that i sensed my situation
that i created something
out of my situation
out of my life
that i lived
as human
alive
i

i died 26 july 1999 on the costa do sol
i found myself in a situation

i died 26 july 1999 in the grasslands
i found myself in a situation

i died 26 july 1999 in the kgalagadi
i found myself in a situation

i died 26 july 1999 in an argument
i found myself in a situation

CRY ME A RIVER

who's that rowing a black boat
through this black night?

who's that not sparing his arms
and rowing without end?

who's that rowing a boat
on the river without an end?
who's that not giving up hope
on a journey without end?

who's that rowing a black boat
black in the black night?
who's that hearing the slavebell
and beating the thud of his gut?

OUR KING

1

we prayed for the welfare of our king
we were his humble children
we danced for our kingdom
we did not have a greater king
we kept little ice statues of him in our fridges

but now the barbarians are here
they find our little ice statues amusing
and good enough to keep their drinks cool

2

then our king was dethroned
now he lives in a small back room
the windows are plastered over
his psychiatrist comes daily
to treat him for his schizophrenia
otherwise he sings hymns

or pages through the bible
that is always on a pedestal next to his bed
lying ready and waiting just like the mouse
waits to bite the cat to death

translated from the Afrikaans by Karen Press

MY HANDS

my hands are dead turned yellow

i stand alone
alone at the end of the road
my open hands
open at your door

my skull explodes
explodes with hands and all
my skull
with my hands inside

once my hands were birds singing

CONFIDENTIALLY YOURS

1

my lord
i know my presence irritates you
i want to enter your house
and page through your thesis
and have a drink with you
and have a chat
and have a laugh

and smoke a pipe with you
and tap you on the shoulder
i am waiting at your door
i'll wait, i'll keep on waiting
    my lord

2

serowe general dealers (pty.) ltd.

a grimace this scape and you
and here could be anywhere
a khotla yonder under big tree
and old men raising hell their skulls
a woman, oh women of my village
a clear yell, a spilt otsogile
and here could be anywhere
a lone goat thorns its eyes, mud hut
a morukuru tree bleaches sun
and we are everyone

home shop is your shop – tsena!

3

    !kick that black dog

i caught some white insects
i tied them to a tin carriage

they are hauling gold from hell
they are kidding themselves silly

cause i got them all tied up
cause they graft it out all day

sometimes they go all haywire
sometime i will die laughing

!kick that black dog

NOW THAT IT'S TOO LATE

I'll wait till the shrill yellow sun
explodes gasping over the mountains
then, against the flaming morning
I'll make the tokoloshe pray
that the distant crackle of bombfire
beats sense into bent black backs
until, late at eventide
the moon, a bowl of blood, trots
sacredly through the heavens laughing
at baas's meaningless joke
yes, I know his voice well –
just like the nightly tot dance

now that the thistle screams wildly
I know where my salvation lies –
buried deep beneath stone and bulb
where my ancestral oxen
are chased by tanks
that leave me transfixed with hate
and I know, this bloodsoil
is mine and no word or law
will hobble my tokoloshe
here, among our crops, baas
where daily my sickle reaps
here is the battlefield, do you hear me

the corn bullet, the stone grenade
without doubt – I have few words

and I feel bells pealing in my blood
the moment is overripe, its rotten fruit
softens, crushed under my heel
remember now, now that it's too late
I sow bullets over the fields
where now the thistle plumes: sacred

translated from the Afrikaans by Karen Press and Ansie Cilliers

MY BROTHER

as clear as day i remember
my younger brother –
he left home one morning
and never came back

i remember we went to the river
i saw his body sleeping
deep under the water
i did not cry –

but i remember his quiet face
as he lay in his coffin
his nose and mouth stuffed
with clean cotton wool

i remember i was not surprised
when i saw him a week later
greeting me from amidst the crowd
at the market of our village

1

we all sat roun a faia
a cops
squadcar holler a stop
a lump
a fool we dont run but
sit an
grin.hell,Lod,i saw 'm
thump da nightwatch down
his head a ball o' blood
i a white:we dont want
to see
you here again. an what
dat ma
bitch scuttled roun da
cona. i
my pals all gone,o Lod

2

i saw her sit on a sidewalk
i saw her spit blood in a gutter
i saw her stump for a foot
i saw her clutch a stick
i saw her eyes grin toothless
i saw thorns in her burnt flesh

i see her cut her own throat
i see her corpse lie in Dark City
i see her save a multitude

3

on my way to St. Peter's Gate
i see a sign looming up –

WELCOME TO SOWETO:
air-conditioned rooms with baths
we can recommend the soap –

4

he sits in glory
a red robe
a golden throne
a thorn crown
the halo
the cross
the works

on his farm
khaki shorts
chev truck
barbed wire
smoke ring
fencing pole
the works

5

today is tuesday
yesterday was monday
tomorrow will be wednesday
after that another day

time after time the sea
collapses to certain death
on its burning beaches

time after time our prime
minister proclaims lasting peace
and nails sharpeville on
another burning cross

today is dingaan's day
yesterday was republic day
tomorrow will be an ordinary day
after that a similar day

"A TOOTH DRESSED UP IN JACKBOOTS . . . "

A tooth dressed up in jackboots
And a bow-tie; it polished
The white enamel of its face
It stamped, it clicked
It denied it was rotten
It salivated, it drooled for more
It bit into the curve of the world.

"SOMETIMES THE MOUTH'S A LOCKED CELL . . . "

Sometimes the mouth's a locked cell.
In solitary confinement, it has nothing to say.
Its teeth are the enamel gaolers
Letting nothing in, nothing out.
The tongue grows long and lean.
Then the silent mouth cell grows hungry.
It waters. It would like to suck out
The juice of a word,
It would like to bite into the flesh
Of vowels and syllables
And fling their gnawed bones around.
But the mouth's got nothing to say
For itself now;
It's deafdumb. It has no alphabet.
The tongue is long and lean.
It can only sit out the days of waiting
Behind clenched gaoler teeth.

THE BULLET

What are these roots doing with my hair?
What are these stones doing with my nails?
What is this dark soil doing with my thirst?

The bullet whistled through my hand, and sang
Of my little girl whom I had held tight,
Her blonde hair, her chameleon eyes;
The bullet whistled through my head and I could
Feel the hole there, my memory leaking out,
And yet my wife was at my side, holding
Me for comfort in her thighs.
We throbbed together, blood glued to one another

                   . . . and I was left alone
In the stinging dark, an ape at my head, tearing with his
Paws into my wound, and the pain so dreadful
That even the stars dived underground,
And I thought of the moon
Mutilated like a cow in the abattoir.

What are these roots doing with my hair?
What are these stones doing with my nails?
What is this dark soil doing with my thirst?

VILLAGES

Steep up the mountain
The heart's ladder
And the heart's panting.

Down below lie the cornfields
And the villages of words.

We've left the villages far behind
The words can no longer be said,
Can no longer express.

Instead, the solemn silence
Broken by the fart of a goat.

Steep up the mountain
The heart's ladder
And the heart's pant
And we've left the villages of words
Far behind.

ICE FLOES

Deep down the ice splits.
The floes are cracking,
The ice floes of the ear.

Hear the slow seeping
Of sea dew
The bark of the sea leopard
The splash of the penguin set free.

The floes are opening,
The ice floes of the ear.

" H E   L A Y   W I T H   H E R   .   .   . "

He lay with her
But she fled from his unfamiliar arms
To hide herself in shadow

So he became a shadow
She camouflaged herself with leaves
So he became a bird
She hurried into the meekness of a cow
So he became a roaring bull
She lay silent in a wheatfield
So he became the reaper
She slipped away from him
As water over stones
So he built an ark
She caught the night
So he shone on her like the moon
She hastened into a girdle of bones
And a soft dress of flesh
So he became a man.

Njabulo S. Ndebele

[BE GENTLE]

Be gentle gentle on [my mind]
please do be gentle,
soft ;
do not crowd my mind
with studied images of my past
let me feel it first :
do not display my carved rituals
at the British Museum,
for little do they say ;
let me feel them first.

It is the fairy tale in me,
[the story book]
that is the pure tale of my being.
Do go gentle on my mind,
softly please,
soft.

THE REVOLUTION OF THE AGED

[my voice is the measure of my life]
it cannot travel far now,
small mounds of earth already bead my open grave,
so come close
    lest you miss the dream.

grey hair has placed on my brow
the verdict of wisdom
and the skin-folds of age
[bear tales] wooled in the truth of proverbs:
if you cannot master the wind,
flow with it
letting know all the time that you are resisting.

75

that is how i have lived
quietly
{ swallowing both the [fresh and foul]
from the mouth of my masters;
yet i watched and listened.

i have listened too
to the condemnations of the young
who burned with scorn
        loaded with revolutionary maxims
            hot for quick results.

they did not know
that their anger
was born in the meekness
with which i whipped my self:
it is blind [progeny]
that acts without indebtedness to the past.

listen now,
the dream:
{ ⏜was playing music on my flute
when a man came and asked to see my flute
and i gave it to him,
but he took my flute and walked away.
i followed this man, asking for my flute;
he would not give it back to me.
{ how i planted vegetables in his garden!
    cooked his food!
how i cleaned his house!
how i washed his clothes
    and polished his shoes!
but he would not give me back my flute,
yet in my [humiliation]
i felt the growth of strength in me
for i had a goal

76

as firm as life is endless,
while he lived in the [darkness of his wrong]

now he has grown hollow from the grin of his cruelty
he kisses death through my flute
which has grown heavy, too heavy
for his withered hands,
and now i should smite him
in my hand is the [weapon of youth.]

do not eat an unripe apple
its bitterness is a tingling knife.
Suffer yourself to wait
and the ripeness will come
and the apple will fall down at your feet.

now is the time
pluck the apple
and feed the future with its ripeness.

THE MAN OF SMOKE

Strapped to my aunt's back
I find warmth.
We walk through many streets
I don't know which,
but I know when we turn.
Even in my blanket,
I can feel the dust of the wind
pecking at me, like many needles,
but I cling to my aunt,
her back is warm and moist.

There are voices in this house
I don't know which,

I'm in the warm darkness
of my blanket.
"Mzalwane" voices greet.
"Bazalwane" auntie answers.
Then I am unstrapped
to the gaze of silence
to the gloom of a candle
to the frightening stares
of a huge face of a person of wood
with teeth as big as fingers
smoke comes out of his mouth,
smoke comes out of his wicked smile.

Put me back, auntie, put me back,
it is cold here
but my words are not lips
they are my hands
clutching at her dress.

She puts me under a table,
but I move out to a corner.
A drum begins the beat:
GOGOM GOM . . . . . GOGOM GOM . . . . .
and there is song and dance
wild song and dance
and I am watching alone
from a corner; my corner.
I am wide eyed
I am shorter than the table
and dancing legs are massive pillars.
I cling to my corner
lest I am crushed by dance.

I cling to my corner
watching my aunt do funny things;
she is mad, quite mad:

all are mad here,
and smoke issues out of
the ugly person's mouth,
smoke is filling the room,
the room is grey smoke now,
GOGOM GOM . . . . . GOGOM GOM . . . . .
Alleluya! Alleluya . . . . .

round round round they dance
round the table
GOGOM GOM . . . . . GOGOM GOM . . . . .
Alleluya! Alleluya . . . . .

I am a child watching
from a corner
I am a child clinging
to my corner
I am a child fearing
to be crushed.
I watch my aunt who is mad
quite mad.
All are mad here.
They kneel before the face of smoke
they cry, they shriek,
they breathe in gasps
they say a wind must enter them

they are mad quite mad,
rising to sing and dance and clap hands.
I fear.
I fear people with the wind, praying
like a cow bellowing.

Strapped to my aunt's back,
I find warmth
we walk through many streets

I don't know which,
but I know we are going home now.
I know that we are passing other people
singing, drumming and hand-clapping
down the street:
"These are the wicked dogs
who broke away from our sect.
"Curse them, God. May they burn."
Even in the noise of the wind
I can hear auntie's spitum
cursing the dogs on the tarred road.

But I am warm in the blanket,
it is dark and warm and moist inside,
and I dream of the man of wood
standing next to my bed in the dark,
choking me with his smoke.
And I cry;
"Poor boy, you are hungry" auntie says.

Mbuyiseni Oswald Mtshali

BOY ON A SWING

Slowly he moves
to and fro, to and fro,
then faster and faster
he swishes up and down.

His blue shirt
billows in the breeze
like a tattered kite.

The world whirls by:
east becomes west,
north turns to south;
the four cardinal points
meet in his head.

  Mother!
Where did I come from?
When will I wear long trousers?
Why was my father jailed?

MEN IN CHAINS

The train stopped
at a country station,

Through sleep-curtained eyes
I peered through the frosty window,
and saw six men:
men shorn
of all human honour
like sheep after shearing,
bleating at the blistering wind,

"Go away! Cold wind! Go away!
Can't you see we are naked?"

They hobbled into the train
on bare feet,
wrists handcuffed,
ankles manacled
with steel rings like cattle at the abattoirs
shying away from the trapdoor.

One man with a head
shaven clean as a potato
whispered to the rising sun,
a red eye wiped by a tattered
handkerchief of clouds,
"Oh! Dear Sun!
Won't you warm my heart
with hope?"
The train went on its way to nowhere.

AMAGODUKA AT GLENCOE STATION

We travelled a long journey
through the wattle forests of Vryheid,
crossed the low-levelled Blood River
whose water flowed languidly
as if dispirited for the
shattered glory of my ancestors.

We passed the coalfields of Dundee –
blackheads in the wrinkled face
of Northern Zululand –
until our train ultimately came
to a hissing stop at Glencoe.

Many people got off
leaving the enraged train
to snort and charge at the night
on its way to Durban.

The time was 8 p.m.
I picked up my suitcase,
sagging under the weight of a heavy overcoat
I shambled to the 'non-European Males' waiting room

The room was crowded
the air hung, a pall of choking odour,
rotten meat, tobacco and sour beer.

Windows were shut tight
against the sharp bite of winter.

Amagoduka sat on bare floor
their faces sucking the warmth
of the coal fire crackling in the corner.

They chewed dried bread
scooped corned beef with rusty knives,
and drank mqombothi from the plastic can
which they passed from mouth to mouth.

They spoke animatedly
and laughed in thunderous peals.

A girl peeped through the door,
they shuddered at the sudden cold blast,
jumped up to fondle and leer at her.

Hau! ngena Sis – Oh! come in sister!

She shied like a frightened filly
banged the door and bolted.

They broke into a tumultuous laughter.

One of them picked up a guitar
plucked it with broken fingernails
caressed its strings with a castor oil bottle –

it sighed like a jilted girl,
"You play down! Phansi! Play D" he whispered.

Another joined in with a concertina,
its sound fluttered in flowery notes
like a butterfly picking pollen from flower to flower.

The two began to sing,
their voices crying for the mountains
and the hills of Msinga, stripped naked of
their green garment.

They crossed rivers and streams,
gouged dry by the sun rays,
where lowing cattle genuflected
for a blade of grass and a drop of water
on riverbeds littered with carcasses and bones.

They spoke of hollow-cheeked maidens
heaving drums of brackish water
from a far away fountain.

They told of big-bellied babies
sucking festering fingers
instead of their mothers' shrivelled breasts.

Two cockroaches
as big as my overcoat buttons
jived across the floor
snatched meat and bread crumbs
and scurried back to their hideout.

The whole group joined in unison:
various eyes peered through frosted windows
"Ekhaya bafowethu! – Home brothers!"

THE DETRIBALISED

He was born in Sophiatown,
Or Alexandra, I am not sure,
but certainly not in Soweto.

He skipped school
during playtime
to hock sweets,
peanuts, shoelaces,
pilfered in town,
caddied at the golfcourse.

He can write –
only his name;
He can read –
The World:
"Our one and only paper,"
The Golden City Post –
murder, rape and robbery.

He has served time
at the "Fort."
Prison is no shame,
just as unavoidable
and unpleasant
as going to a dentist.

He's a "clever"
not a "moegie";

he never says baas
to no bloody white man.

He wears
the latest Levison's suits
"Made in America";
from Cuthbert's
a pair of Florsheim shoes
"America's finest shoes"
He pays cash
that's why
he's called Mister.

He goes for quality, man,
not quantity, never –
the price is no obstacle.

His furniture is
from Ellis, Bradlow's, exclusive.

Nothing from the O.K. Bazaars
except groceries
and Christmas toys
for their kids.
"Very cheap!" says his wife.

Yes, his wife –
also born in the city, Orlando!
she's pretty,
dresses very well:
costumes from Vanité or Millews.

She's very sophisticated,
uses Artra, Hi – Lite
skin lightening cream,
hair straightened,

wears lipstick
a wig, nail polish:
she can dance
the latest "Monkey."

He married her
after he had fathered
two kids
to prove her fertility.
There's the occasional
domestic quarrel:
he punches her
a "blue eye"
to show her
he's the boss.

He takes another cherie
to the movies
at Lyric or Majestic.
They dine at the Kapitan
and sleep at the Planet.

Maybe they go
to a night session
in a posh shebeen:
jazz, booze
knives and guns.

The wife sees
a "nyanga"
to bring her man back home

He runs a car –
'60 Impala Chev.
Automatic, sleek.

He knows
he must carry a pass.
He don't care for politics
He don't go to church
He knows Sobukwe
he knows Mandela
They're in Robben Island.
"So what? That's not my business!"

TALISMANS

Bring me a locust
to fry until its skin turns brown;
the broiled serrated legs exude green marrow,
the tips of a million sunrays stored
in lifeless eyes;
the wings will stay frayed at the edges.

Give me a stripped rat to skin,
I'll rip its tiny belly open.
The trickle of blood will smudge my fingers;
I'll fashion its fangs into a necklace.
"A choker of evil spirits!"

Let me have the feathers of an owl,
plucked clean of its vaunted wisdom,
the fluffy down stripped into nakedness,
the indicator of arid yesterday,
the pointer to a bleak tommorow.

Who will offer me
a few quills of a fat porcupine?
Their sharpness will prick the deadwood,
the hidebound souls of hypocrites;

to prise open the undeciphered scrolls
of vile deeds committed over past centuries.

The tests are predictable.
The results will be positive.

Mandla Langa

THE PENSION JIVEASS

I lead her in,
A sepia figure 100 years old.
Blue ice chips gaze
And a red slash gapes:
'What does she want?'
I translate: "Pension, sir."
"Useless kaffir crone,
Lazy as the black devil.
She'll get fuck-all."
I translate.
"My man toiled
And rendered himself impotent
With hard labour.
He paid tax like you.
I am old enough to get pension.
I was born before the great wars
And saw my father slit your likes' throats!"
I don't translate, but
She loses her pension anyhow.

DEATH OF THE MINERS *OR* THE WIDOWS OF
THE EARTH

We waited in silence for our children
Their voices wounded the earth.
It was as if our very footsteps
Crushed their last breath of life

The final day came . . .
Our village was a forest of new comers and goers
Decorations were suspended on high poles of the village.
Men with polished shoes and women with high-pitched voices
Paraded the streets like some freshly fed peacocks
Yes! Bells, voices, sirens:
"THE LEADER has arrived"
Proclaimed the carefully woven banners
Only then and only then did we know the fate of our men . . .

Life continues unchanged in our village
Men still leave early at dawn.
Silence walks where once was the pomp of yesterday.
Old tattered flags hang on the side-streets
Only us and the memory of pain remain
We are the widows of the earth
We are the orphans of stone
Insanity stares unblinkingly through the broken windows.

Those who waited in the night of the earth
Until their eyes succumbed to the darkness
Until they bellowed with mocking laughter,
Until they lived the illusion of escape;
They were our fathers, our husbands and our children.

On that day, on that morning

The last words were spoken softly on the doorsteps
The air was cold
The farewells were long.

News travels fast these days
Suddenly our village was invaded by whiskered men
By those who spoke for us to yet others
Who spoke for us.
They clucked in a language that was foreign to us.

These were Publicmen and Writers
And men of substance who make money and interviews.
Some spoke casually to us
Until told we were the wives and children of "Them."
Then they came closer to us to dissect our feelings
To know how we had spent the night.

They did not remember
We had seen them that very day
Talking wisely for us in those boxes.
From their words you would have thought
They knew all the buried truths of our husbands' terrors
In truth to know so much is a gift of divining.

translated from the Zulu by the poet

THE POLITICAL PRISONER

I desired to talk
And talk with words as numerous as sands,
The other side of the wire,
The other side of the fortress of stone.

I found a widow travelling
Passing the prisoners with firewood.

It is this woman who forbade me to sleep
Who filled me with dreams.

The dream is always the same.
It turns on an anchor
Until it finds a place to rest:
It builds its cobwebs from the hours.

One day someone arrives and opens the gate.
The sun explodes its fire
Spreading its flames over the earth,
Touching the spring of mankind.

Behind us there are mountains
Where the widow is abandoned.
She remains there unable to give birth
Priding herself only in the shadows of yesterdays.

translated from the Zulu by the poet

THE TYRANT

Through uncertainty the tyrant imposes his power.
He chooses the gods that speak his own language,
To make us stand before him like cattle.
By his ancestral names he haunts our children.
They must parade at his festivals like slaves
To declaim the glories of his violent prophets.
The enemy boasts the power of the sun,
The beast steals the young from their mother's breast,
The tyrant celebrates, the feast is in his name . . .

translated from the Zulu by the poet

We erred too, we who abandoned our household gods
And raised theirs with soft skins and iron flesh.
Their priests made signs at our forefathers' grounds
They spoke in a language that was obscure to us.
To win their praise we delivered our children,
But their lips were sealed and without the sacred mark.
Tired of obscurity they invaded our earth,
Plundering the minds of our captured children.
Yet nothing was so foolish as to burn the symbols of our gods.
Then, to follow helplessly the bubblings of their priests
We emulated their ridiculous gestures and earned their laughter.
Now, we dare not celebrate our feast unless purified by fire
Unless our minds are nourished by the Ancestral Song.
We have vowed through the powers of our morning:
We are not the driftwood of distant oceans.
Our kinsmen are a thousand centuries old.
Only a few nations begat a civilization
Not of gold, not of things, but of people.

translated from the Zulu by the poet

TO MY FRIEND SOLOMON HAILU

And so, you my friend must forgive me;
You who saw the movement of my breath,
Who saw the ugliness of giving birth.
O! my friend it is not true that a child is born beautiful;
A child is born ugly, it is born old
It is born wrinkled like an old! lady.
Like a crippled old man,
But those who love her still embrace the ugliness.
I am grateful always for your presence at the lake,
You continued to dream,

You must tell them about the dream.
Tell them, a dream does not begin as a dream,
But as a nightmare.
Yet as time upturns, as time unveils itself,
A rainbow image spins wide through the sky.
And you my friend you beheld my death,
So you must forgive.
A friend must not see the death of a friend.
And yet my friend, I had to die.
I had to die, to enter into the flames of my future times.

translated from the Zulu by the poet

Sheila Cussons

CLOTHED NAKEDNESS

A blaze wear I
between the world and my blood
more mine, more my own than anything
a without-name
that, to destroy
would be the destruction of me:
o intolerable, tender, defenceless shirt of flame.

translated from the Afrikaans by Johann de Lange

ORGAN

My senses are interchangeable,
hear colours, listen to smells:
scarlet blares, pepper is a pizzicato
and brown is a rumble of drums.
And summer, summer especially, sweeps
through the nose: sun is seething lye.
Wool-oil of hot air surprises me,
like the sweat of warriors when onions
steam in a pot. And there is someone
so acutely, sensuously alive
that asleep he is nutmeg and luke-warm milk,
and awake, blazing August
in a cicada pine grove. And each
season chooses its senses –
winter is pure ear – and mingles them again
until each in each recognises the other,
and thronging with creatures
complexly contrapuntal, around
the round year the great Te Deum
resounds with all the stops out.

translated from the Afrikaans by the poet

The pigsty did not reek:
it smelled pleasantly crass-sour-rotten,
and the gluttonous snouts in hogwash and gourd
and the unmentionable mud was the most wonderful
most daring bad manners imaginable –
I loved the pigsty far removed
at the lower end of the barn-yard,
behind a row of cypresses, and liked to sit on its wall
to sniff in deeply the feral scent
and be amazed at animals so shamelessly
gluttonous they even guzzle with their snouts;
and their ugly heavy mugs with the stupid
white-eyelashed eyelets like something from Grimm
or Anderson. Indeed, the pigs were Somebodies,
like princes disguised by withered old witches
or Circe's swine-sailors –
Nearly sun-blind I dreamt about them,
until mud mellow, so strong and richly sweet
saturated my young veins the magical enchantment
of all the summers of my youth –
Back in the house:
Good Lord one really cannot bear this
Grandmother piously complained about the heat
and, hell but it's hot, bluntly
from my slightly more carnal mother:
how could they understand that the scorching day
and the pigsty
was a heaven to me, a fable unrivalled –
Also the lost paradise was just outside the house:
a big old plum – tree with sinful fruit
which fell from above just like us,
and if you picked one up you could still see in time
how the evil quickly recoiled
back into the injured flesh –

O lost barn-yard, in you I could find the whole Old Testament
and the Greek legends and Anderson.

YELLOW GRAMOPHONE

Hello, daffodil, saffron-yellow exclamation,
whirligig, little windmill,
an old-fashioned gramophone horn.
And I feel my mama dancing again
to the swing of twenty-two,
and I, through membrane,
conscious of a submarine glow –
the lamps glitter – the pulsation
and mermaid song of drums and saxophone,
until, exhilarated, I let go
and race my little feet along with mama.

You are beautiful, daffodil, out of
the dark earth, the silent, cold dark earth –

Hello, goodbye, yellow gramophone.

PEARL

The silent black oyster formed me white.
I am the bitter bright grain,
the hard distress in her astonished flesh,
but ever more tightly fear fastens
her muscles round me, for she prefers

to that other anguish
my alien gnawing in her side.

translated from the Afrikaans by the poet

Wilma Stockenström

AFRICA LOVE

Like Inhaca facing the coast, I'm turned
to you, with my soft mouth, my breasts.
Like her I nestle in a bay of kindness,
I grow, coral-like but without fail
closer to you, my mainland.
What does the mercantile marine back
on the battering seas mean to me?
Cunningly my dripping mangroves advance
in tepid waters step by little step.
How long before I merge with your wide
cashew-nut forests, before we fit into each other,
your reed-overgrown arm around me,
your brown body my body.

translated from the Afrikaans by Johann de Lange

EAST COAST

Curled up, woman with cancerous cities
like broken crabs in her breasts
making her milk seep into the ground
to curdle sweetly into white
roots, the east coast lies asleep.
Into hollows of mouldering a moisture of ants
oozes from between her thighs.
She is the lovely fertile corpse,
her eyelids mottled leaves,
steadily decaying into tree or building,
into industry's smoking nostrils.
From semen so lavishly wasted on her,
amid the steely canes of cranes,
there sprouts the new youth, a foot-stamping
thousand, beating the shields of their chests,

shouting: Africa!
Africa out of a toadstool woman's navel.

translated from the Afrikaans by Johann de Lange

K O I C H A B ' S   W A T E R

Seven thousand years' accumulated softness
I draw from a tap for the daily
chore of washing nylons and drip-dry things.
Then to the kitchen to move pots and pans about
and pour water on sticky crusts.

When this water first saw the light
it briefly wondered why precisely then.

Then through underground pipes it
flowed and up to all the proper places

with its matchless whiteness to purify
and refresh and humbly become part
of brandy and water, of waste, and sewage:
a woman of noble disposition
giving herself, simply, without asking.

translated from the Afrikaans by Johann de Lange

T H E   R O C K

Sat down beside a grandfather
of a rock, by chance, and breathed
mouldiness of fungus and spore.
How, I wonder, does one measure
a rock? Where, more or less, does

a rock start, and where does
a rock end, like the one I'm leaning against?
Rocks are for all. Snail-trails
and gossamer plugs in little hollows
indicate that my rock serves as tavern,
and that I, had I the strength
to roll it over with a sturdy pole,
would find an even burrow for a snake,
or ant-eggs white like grains of rice.

The rock shows its face to the world.
It has no hands to cover
its face, it depends on my kindness.
Wide awake, yet defenceless, the rock
lies listening whether I mean it harm.
It has no mouth to scare me away.
One would think it quite meek.

Rocks sometimes are keepers of fossils,
of ammonites, like something nascent
in a body of rock; of leaves
pressed to mere semblances of themselves;
of prophetic fish-symbols; of skulls
and the knuckle-bones of carnivores.
Rocks are treasure-troves of crystals.
Rocks crammed with a splintery splendour
glow passionately as if seaweed petrified,
as if a chrysanthemum hardened
inside them charging them with the colour
of deserts and vygies, the horror colours
of the eerie night-art of dreams,
and the red of reflectors.

My rock, my rock, tell me in your muteness
what you guard. Tell me
whether you knew youth, and was your middle age

brittle and sheer, burnished
and rubbed to purest carat?
Or is being rock being old,
is it having been old, is it knowing
oldness? Is being old being rock, hard,
but exposed to kicks and weathering?

Rock, my rock, the blueheaded lizard
watches over you! The shrubs warm you!
The sand dusts a blanket over you!
The snail drapes you with silver chains
and the spider nurses you!
I shall return.

translated from the Afrikaans by Johann de Lange

CONFESSION OF A GLOSSY STARLING

Slipping from darkness to godliness,
as quickly stripped of splendour, I,
hopping about, try to show my colours.
In the glossy starling-shifting
from lustre to oblivion
I lose delight in hopelessly
– starling this, starling that – being me.

Always alighting from the branch
to pander one's precocity,
pecking next to sandals and velschoen,
remaining starling this, starling that
of oblivion, lustre; never to
stop yearning for the final surrender
to blue and green and feather-turned flame.

In my glossy starling confession
I hop from truth illuminated

to obscure darkness and mischief,
I sparkle with gaudy feathers,
my speech petulant and tedious
and complain and confess and remain
bird of lustre and of oblivion.

translated from the Afrikaans by Johann de Lange

THE SKULL LAUGHS THOUGH THE FACE CRIES

One day, I know, I'll outface
death with grinning skull. At least
I'll retain my sense of humour. But
whether, like the late Mrs. Ples
or the blue buck of my native land,
I'll warrant a glass case in a museum . . . ?
Man is not exactly a rare animal.

Still, how clever we are with our
inner clockwork-genius, how strong
the wide swaying crane-like gestures
with which we drop rectangular skyscrapers
in residential areas and business centres.
Remarkable our scrambling research
right through dolomite to sink our arms
shaft-deep to grab and haul up
the grey ore, grinding
and refining it to bar on bar of hive-like
packed safes of investments. Oh yes,
absolutely marvellous our ability to enrich
discarded sand to fire-dust
which, if we wanted to, might just
furiously, beautifully burn up everything
in an ultimate unrepeatable blaze.

Didn't I say the skull laughs
though the face cries?

translated from the Afrikaans by Johann de Lange

HOUSEBREAKING OF THE MAMBA

The mamba slings its thong-thin yards
round the house on the hill of the watershed,
swiftly winds its rubbery bands
round the upright barrel, two-storeyed.
Its listening tongue probes, tries the keyhole,
the burglar-proofing. Next, on tiled asbestos roof,
down the chimney it nimbly thrusts itself
and gleaming blackly glides down sooty darkness

Now the siren wails over houses crouching
behind flowery hedges where the roads fork.
Doors of courthouses slam shut, the veil
of the temple of money tears.
In lecture halls the lights go out. In warm
shafts the water surges, glistening, flows
rippling over the gold-warted city.

Its task completed, the mamba swings
itself up, straight, next to the bed, stares
with stony eye at the man parting the waters,
and lays its cold chin on the pale throat.

translated from the Afrikaans by Johann de Lange

THREE SECTIONS FROM CHRISTMAS IN AFRICA

In the House of the Father

Christmas, the turning time, the final reckoning and the
forgiveness, we rode towards each year, over humps of
bitterness, towards the father

omnipotent and bountiful night rider with his magical
reindeer and sack full of gifts –
you could rely on him always to be there when you got there

accept the culmination of your year in his lap
hear all, forgive with a wish, and let you
begin all over;

a time of reprieve and new resolutions, time when you could
believe in new beginnings, a time of peace and long
playtime. With a hand in the dark

it began before dawn. The sun would rise over the city
as we passed the last gold hills of the mine dumps. Always
I saw children leaping up them, and in my head, in golden depths

a heap of little skeletons. Then the long hot hours dreaming
through the dorps each its single tree and tin roofs blazing
each its lone dog barking and black silent men

propped on the verandah of the general store, drinking
lemonade. Endless car games, the singing game chanting every
    rhyme we knew
from ten green bottles to jesus loves me over the veld

to pass the time. At last, crossing, purple and lonely
the valley of a thousand hills, the tropical
deep smell of heavy flowers would glut the evening

and my father offered sixpence for the first to see the sea.
And there it was after a sudden unbending – that immense blue
    promise.
Then inland into the sugar cane in the deep of night

the rustle of dunes and the sugar cane fields
the farmers who kept pythons fifty feet long to keep the rats
    down
and at midnight

the cottage. O the damp smell of foliage, smell of salt
and the sea's heavy breathing in the night, stray cries
of live things, batswing, shadows, sleep, and a ring of mornings.

The snakes were the price. In their hundreds they inhabited
our world at christmas. They were the hazard
in the garden. And they were everywhere

tangled in undergrowth, slithering over your feet in the pathway
stretched across doorways in the sun
lurking under the banana plant and nesting in the luckybean tree

they were everywhere, everywhere. And happiness was
    everywhere
in the father's time, who came down from heaven
in his red dressing gown and my father's shoes at the appointed
    time

cottonwool beard lopsided across his grin
his arms full of parcels.
His was the future that always came, keeping its promise.

In the house of the father the year would turn
a flower full blown, shedding its petals.
Glistened in your hand a free gift, a clean seed.

The Punishment

One autumn afternoon when I was nine
feeding the chickens near the grapevine, brooding
in sunshine, my mother asked me to choose

a christmas present that year.
Anything I said, but a doll. Whatever you choose
but not a doll

my faith in her to know
better than I could myself what gift would please me.
And so at the height of summer

we made our pilgrimage
to the earth's greenest riches and the ample ocean.
And christmas eve

was three white daughters
three bright angels singing silent night as my mother
lit the candles

the tree blooming
sea breathing, the beloved son in his cradle sleeping.
Over the hills and skies

on his sleigh the father
the awaited one, made his visitation. Weeks of dreaming
and wondering now

in a box in my hand.
Shoebox size. Not waterwings then or a time machine no
something the size

of a pair of shoes.
Not a pony then or a river canoe. Not a new dress no.
I pulled at the bright bowed ribbons

and little christmas angels
with trembling hands. Underneath the monkey-apple branch
dressed up in baubles and tinsel

and blobs of cotton wool
the sea roaring, stars and the fairy at the treetop
shining

his hand on my shoulder
my mother's eyes on my face two burning suns
piercing my mind and in the box

a doll.
A stupid pretty empty thing. Pink smiling girl. The world
rocked about my head

my face fell into a net
from that moment. My heart in me played possum
and never recovered.

I said I liked the wretched thing
joy broke over my face like a mirror cracking. I said it
so loud, so often

I almost believed it. All that christmas
a shameful secret bound me and the doll and my mother
irrevocably together.

When I knew she was watching
I would grab for the doll in the night, or take it
tenderly with me to the beach

wrapped in a small towel.
At last on the last night of the journey home
staying at a hotel

my mother woke me early
to go out and find the maid. In my pyjamas, half asleep
I staggered out into the dawn

heat rising like mist
from the ground, birds making an uproar, snakes
not yet awake

a sense of something
about to happen under the heavy damp rustle
of the trees.

My feel left footprints
in the dew. When I returned I was clutching that precious
corpse to my chest

like one of the bereaved.
Now I know, said my mother, that although you didn't
want a doll, you really do love her.

I was believed!
Something fell from my face with a clatter –
my punishment was over

and in that moment
fell from my mother's face a particular smile, a kind of
dear and tender curling of the eyes

fell. Two gripped faces
side by side on the floor, smiled at each other
before we grabbed them back

and fitted them with a hollow rattle
to our love. And I laid the doll down in a suitcase
and slammed the lid on its face

and never looked at it again.
And in a sense my mother did the same, and in a sense
my punishment and hers

had always been, and just begun.

The Kiss

Out of a jungle of dreams
at the first creak of morning, the house still dark and
softly breathing

out I went creeping
into the first light of morning where the mighty Puff Adder
at the edge of the verandah

just out of sight
in his rightful place was lying in wait for me
ready to strike.

My first leap of the day
carried me over and beyond him as I turned mid air in my flight
to greet him

he was gone.
O master invisible. Scent of undergrowth
scent of white transparent flowers

sweet and stinging
mist from the tangle of green and fresh sea smell
struck my brain.

Under the luckybean tree
gathering good luck in my basket
I met the Night Adder

master of darkness O beautiful
your fangs inches from my face suddenly flung up mighty
I embrace you

I flee
but the darkness has opened in me, is answering
answering

all night I lie coiled in your exquisite body
my eyes tight shut. If I wake I'll see the slime
at the corners of your lips

you are held in
tight as a spring, a pot of poison. My reflection
moves on your still surface.

Across pale grass the pathway
curves upward innocent as skin towards the drop
the saltclean ocean.

Yet I come.
You exist. Your mate has nested
in my wrist.

Mamba, emperor of all things green
like fire you have slipped between my thighs
at the edge of the world I stand trembling

my father is slashing and slashing
at a ringhals under the bed with a huge stick. A wild
uncontrollable thing

contracting and flaying the air
cracking and twisting on the floor as we run screaming
from the house as from

a thing immortal.
Who let it in? It's a crisis. We are gathered
to defend something

my mother is nowhere to be seen.
Someone must have let it in. My mother must have let it in.
You give me no rest.

There is something in men's eyes
ritualistic, dangerous, an ancient slit-eyed look
as they file out to hunt you down

my father in the lead
the brave one, his courage on his shoulders
big as a ship.

Yet I come towards you
night after night in my flight from you. You give me no rest
Your mate has nested in my breast.

And so he came unexpectedly
her eyes half closed not to see
he deceived her. It is his nature.

Two small holes in her calf
two fang marks turning blue. Like a burning thing
she is wildly running

she is mad with pain.
His poison in her body swells out
like an inkfish dying.

Her limbs are turning purple and green
she's an exotic flower, a symphony of pain.
Yet I come.

She is lying under a heap
of poison flesh. All around her, eyes
like trees

bend down and surround her
in a shock of tourniquets and syringes, eyes full of
revulsion, of recognition.

This time we are leaving
for good. I am sent to say goodbye to the sea. Immense and blue
it stretches below me

drowns my crying.
I watch it flow towards me without ending.
I feel dry as a nut.

Kneeling at the water's edge
I gather sea water and salt black weed into a jar
a talisman.

My father packs it up in the boot of the car
and drives us away.
My mother carries the poison of a viper in her vein.

We are survivors
we go out into the wilderness. A microbe
resting on the shore of an artery

might hear the heart booming.

Oupa Thando Mthimkulu

LIKE A WHEEL

This thing is like a wheel
It turns
Today it's me
Tomorrow it's you

Today I'm hungry
Tomorrow it's you

Today I'm hungry
Tomorrow it's you
Today I'm homeless
Tomorrow it's you

Today I'm in prison
Tomorrow it's you

This thing is like a wheel

NINETEEN SEVENTY-SIX

Go nineteen seventy-six
We need you no more
Never come again
We ache inside.
Good friends we have
Lost.
Nineteen seventy-six
You stand accused
Of deaths
Imprisonments
Exiles
And detentions.

117

You lost the battle
You were not revolutionary
Enough
We do not boast about you
Year of fire, year of ash.

Motshile Nthodi

STAFFRIDER

Black boy
no recreation centre
no playing grounds
no money for lunch at school
not enough schoolbooks
no proper education
no money for school journeys

but
one Saturday morning
my father gave me
one shilling and six pennies
he said
my son
go and make enough
for a living

With eleven pennies
I bought a return ticket to town
the remaining seven for provision
good enough

I was one of those
carry-boys at the municipal market
caddy at the golf course
selling oranges and peanuts
illegally on the trains

money money money
that's not enough for a boy
what about entertainment

right
I am seventeen by now

waiting on a station platform
waiting for the conductor's
whistle of command
waiting for the train
to roll on its permanent rail

now steel wheels of an electric train
start playing a tune of
percussion and trombone
from the middle of the platform
pulling myself from the crowd
waiting for the tube to the north

like a bebop dancer
I turn around twice
and I open the window
push up the frame with my elbow
grab the frame between
the window and the door

listen to the improvisation
from my dirty oversize
canvas shoes
pha – – phapha – phapha –
pha – phapha – phapha –
phapha – phapha –

listen to the shouting
and whistles
from the audience in that tube
when I swing on the outer handle
and rest on the bottom stair

THAT'S THEATRE HEY

they see me once
but only once

I'm on top of the coach
lying eight inches under
the main power lines

ACROBATIC HEY

they see me once again
but only once
I'm under the coach
lying on a steel frame
next to the wheels

CIRCUS HEY

fifteen stations
stupids packed
sardines in the tube
phapha – pha –
poor black eyes on me
– phapha –
home station
– pha – phapha – phaphaphaphapha

WA SALA WENA

– phaphapha –
railway police chasing me
I jump the platform
the railway line
the fence
across the river
towards home
I'm safe

this is the Saturday programme
and till we meet again

121

thank you brothers and sisters,
thank you.

SOUTH AFRICAN DIALOGUE

Morning Baas,
Baas,
Baas Kleinbaas says,
I must come and tell
Baas that,
Baas Ben's Baasboy says,
Baas Ben want to see
Baas Kleinbaas if
Baas don't use
Baas Kleinbaas,
Baas.

Tell
Baas Kleinbaas that,
Baas says,
Baas Kleinbaas must tell
Baas Ben's Baasboy that,
Baas Ben's Baasboy must tell
Baas Ben that,
Baas says,
If Baas Ben want to see
Baas Kleinbaas,
Baas Ben must come and see
Baas Kleinbaas here.

Thank you
Baas.
I'll tell
Baas Kleinbaas that,

Baas says,
Baas Kleinbaas must tell
Baas Ben's Baasboy that,
Baas Ben's Baasboy must tell
Baas Ben that,
Baas says,
If Baas Ben want to see
Baas Kleinbaas,
Baas Ben must come and see
Baas Kleinbaas here,
Baas.
Goodbye Baas.

Baas Kleinbaas,
Baas says,
I must come and tell
Baas Kleinbaas that,
Baas Kleinbaas must tell
Bass Ben's Baasboy that,
Baas Ben's Baasboy must tell
Baas Ben that,
Baas says,
If Baas Ben want to see
Baas Kleinbaas,
Baas Ben must come and see
Baas Kleinbaas here,
Baas Kleinbaas.

Baasboy,
Tell Baas Ben that,
Baas Kleinbaas says,
Baas says,
If Baas Ben want to see me
(Kleinbaas)
Baas Ben must come and
See me (Kleinbaas) here.

Thank you
Baas Kleinbaas,
I'll tell
Baas Ben that,
Baas Kleinbaas says,
Baas says,
If Baas Ben want to see
Baas Kleinbaas,
Baas Ben must come and see
Baas Kleinbaas here,
Baas Kleinbaas.
Goodbye
Baas Kleinbaas.

Baas Ben,
Baas Kleinbaas says,
I must come and tell
Baas Ben that,
Baas says,
If Baas Ben want to see
Baas Kleinbaas,
Baas Ben must come and see
Baas Kleinbaas there,
Baas Ben.
Baas Ben,
Baas Be-ne . . .
Baas Ben
Goodbye
Baas Ben.

K. Zwide

WOODEN SPOON

I carved a spoon from a rose-root
and, though thornless, its shape was strange,
conforming with the twisted nature
of the rose's journey into the earth.

Grandfather carved a straight spear
of a fine yellow wood;
melted ironstone with oxfat
and beat the blade on a rock,
and, blessing it with leaves and milk,
he whirled it into the air.
In response to gravity
it pierced his heart.

Now I eat with a crooked spoon
which I have dug from my master's garden
and it pierces my heart.

125

Sipho Sepamla

I doesn't care of you black
I doesn't care of you white
I doesn't care of you India
I doesn't care of you kleeling
if sometimes you Saus Afrika
you gotta big terrible terrible
somewheres in yourselves
because why
for sure you doesn't look anader man in da eye

I mean for sure now
all da peoples is make like God
sometimes you wanna knows how I meaning for
is simples
da God I knows for sure
He make avarybudy wit' one heart

for sure now dis heart go-go da same
dats for meaning to say
one man no diflent to anader
so now
you see a big terrible terrible stand here
how one man make anader man feel
da pain he doesn't feel hisself
for sure now dats da whole point

sometime you wanna know how I meaning for
is simples
when da nail of da t'orn tree
scratch little bit little bit of da skin
I doesn't care of say black
I doesn't care of say white
I doesn't care of say India
I doesn't care of say kleeling

I mean for sure da skin
only one t'ing come for sure
and da one t'ing for sure is red blood
dats for sure da same da same
for avarybudy.

Mafika Gwala

GUMBA, GUMBA, GUMBA

Been watching this jive
For too long.
That's struggle.
West Street ain't the place
To hang around any more;
Pavid's Building is gone.
Gone is Osmond's Bottle Store.
And West Street is like dry;
The dry of patent leather
When the guests have left.
And the cats have to roll like
Dice into the passageways . . .
Seeking a fix
While they keep off the jinx.
That's struggle.

Miasmic haze at 12 noon
Stretching into the wilderness
Of uniformed gables . . .
Vast and penetrating
As the Devil's eye.
At night you see another dream
White and monstrous;
Dropping from earth's heaven,
Whitewashing your own Black dream
That's struggle.
Get up to listen
To Black screams outside;
With deep cries, bitter cries.
That's struggle.

Struggle is when
You have to lower your eyes
And steer time

With your bent voice.
When you drag along –
Mechanically.
Your shoulders refusing;
Refusing like a young bull
Not wanting to dive
Into the dipping tank
Struggle is keying your tune
To harmonize with your inside.

Witness a dachshund bitch shitting
A beautiful Black woman's figure too close by,
Her hand holding the strap;
In a whitelonely suburb.
Tramp the city
Even if you're sleepweary;
'Cos your Black arse
Can't rest on a "Whites Only" seat.
Jerk your talk
Frown in your laughs
Smile when you ain't happy.
That's struggle.
Struggle is being offered choices that fink your smiles
Choices that dampen your frown.
Struggle is knowing
What's lacking in your desires
'Cos even your desires are made
To be too hard for you to grab.

Seeing how far
You are from the abyss
Far the way your people are.
Searching your way out
Searching to find it;
Ain't nobody to cry for you.
When you know what's bugging your mama

Your mama coming from the white madam's.
When all the buses
Don't pick you up
In the morning, on your way to work.
'Cos there ain't even room to stand.
Maybe you squeezed all of Soweto,
Umlazi, Kwa-Mashu
Into one stretch of a dream;
Maybe Chatsworth, maybe Bonteheuwel.
Then you chased it & went after it;
It, the IT and ITS.
Perhaps you broke free.
If you have seen:
Seen queues at the off-course tote;
Seen a man's guts – the man walking still
Seen a man blue-eye his wife;
Seen a woman being kicked by a cop.

You seen struggle.
If you have heard:
Heard a man bugger a woman, old as his mother;
Heard a child giggle at obscene jokes
Heard a mother weep over a dead son;
Heard a foreman say "boy" to a labouring oupa
Heard a bellowing, drunken voice in an alley.
You heard struggle.
Knowing words don't kill
But a gun does.
That's struggle.
For no more jive
Evening's eight
Ain't never late.
Black is struggle.

And you once asked why
blacks
    live so fast
    love so fast
    drink so fast
     die so fast
It doesn't start with eMalangeni;
It doesn't.
It starts with the number
you found smeared on the door
        of your home
– and you from school
– or from work.

    one and two
    three and four
    bonk'abajahile

The cement smile
of the teller at the bank
adopted as symbol of courtesy:
    work and save
    wear smart
    get yourself a hi-fi/tv
    buy yourself a car!

    one and two
    three and four
    bonk'abajahile

At Webber's I saw him
running like mad
on a futile marathon
after he'd grabbed a bag

from that farmer
who pronounced "Mophela"
like "amaphela"

I saw her pulling up her pantihose
fixing her semi-Afrowig
With a blue eye and spitting blood
after a fight with another
of Playboy Joe's girls;
Playboy Joe was already at Umgababa
pulling dagga zol with other majitas,
And at Umgababa Alice's Juba
wasn't sour this afternoon.
    one and two
    three and four
    bonk'abajahile

I saw him wave an Okapi
under the Umnqadodo Bridge
to settle scores born of a factory life;
Umgababa's guava tree broke
The guava fruit projectiled
onto Duma's car:
      Hammarsdale 1972.
The knife wound gave the telling of his death.
They covered his body with a Spinlon dustcoat
Waiting for someone to ring Inchanga 41.

    one and two
    three and four
    bonk'abajahile

Langashona's hand against his face
A face long dead to wind the story;
A flower plucked off in bud
Down UNIT ONE SOUTH.

Msingi's expressionless face
A face not squealing.
Bongi Ndlovu
She tried to run, to flee, to plead;
Whick! Whack!
Into flesh came the bushknife
On the sand dunes she collapsed
Waiting for fate to say it's over;
How she let her soul go
is a mystery to bemoan;
Can we blame her kind of life?
Can we blame the rage that held him
in spell?
If we are not saints
They'll try to make us devils;
If we refuse to be devils
They'll want to turn us into robots.
When criminal investigators
are becoming salesmen
When saints are ceasing to be saints
When devils are running back to Hell
It's the Moment of Rise or Crawl
When this place becomes Mpumalanga
With the sun refusing to rise
When we fear our blackness
When we shun our anger
When we hate our virtues
When we don't trust our smiles

      one and two
      three and four
      bonk'abajahile

Sing, how can we sing
      with chainblocks barring us
      the Malombo Sound?

Play, how can we play
  with games turning into nightmares?
Talk, should we not talk with deep open voices?
Wait, should we wait till the cows come home?

KWELA-RIDE

Dompas!
I looked back
Dompas!
I went through my pockets
Not there.

They bit into my flesh (handcuffs).

Came the kwela-kwela
We crawled in.
The young men sang.
In that dark moment

It all became familiar.

TAP-TAPPING

Rough, wet winds
parch my agonized face
as if salting the wounds of
     Bullhoek
     Sharpeville
    Soweto,
unbandage strip by strip
the dressings of Hope;
I wade my senses

through the mist;
I am still surviving
the traumas of my raped soil
alive and aware;
truths jump like a cat leaps for fish
at my mind;
I plod along
  into the vortex
of a clear-borne dawn.

ONE SMALL BOY LONGS FOR SUMMER

for Bill Naughton

The kettle hisses
Mother moves about the kitchen
sliding from corner to corner.
The fire from the stove
pierces into the marrow.
And mother pushing towards the stove
warns of the steam.
My young brother, Thamu, jerks my arm
violently: Stop leaning on me, your elbow
has sunk into my thigh.
            Apology
                I wasn't aware.

The kettle sings
            Some distant far-away song?
Mother picks it up
with an almost tender care.
Sets me thinking of a war-picture
The actor carefully setting the charge
and smiling all the time
                I'll also be a soldier

135

when I'm old – why, Uncle Shoba was one.
Father drops the paper on the table
He comes to join us
            – staring coldly round.
It's no frown really,
But he's grinding his jaws.
            Maybe it's the July
Handicap.

The kettle purrs now
Steam is escaping; it kisses the ceiling
and vanishes. Mother is pouring the violent waters
into the coffee-jug. Coffee.
Yes, I need some coffee – a mug of hot coffee.
Very rousing.
We can't play outside – I must not go, I know
            How we danced in the rain. We are so tired
of the winter: It's so dingy outside.
We can't play inside – I'm so tied up.
It's so boring, I feel like bursting into
a cracking laughter; but father,
he'll go mad.
It's so steamy inside
I feel I could bite the walls down.
If only it makes the winter pass.

IT IS SLEEPY IN THE "COLOURED" TOWNSHIPS

It is sleepy in the "coloured" townships.
The dust clogs in the rheum of every eye
The August winds blow into all the days
Children play in a gust of streets
or huddle in tired dens like a multi-humped camel.

It is sleepy in the "coloured" townships.
Wet washing semaphore, then don't
and the dirt is spiteful to the whiteness
A Volkswagen engine lies embalmed in grease and grime
(the mechanic has washed his hands and left)
but the car waits patient as rust.

It is sleepy in the "coloured" townships.
Heads bob around the stove of the sun
The sleepiness is a crust harder than
a tortoise's shell.

It is sleepy in the "coloured" townships.
A drunk sleeps lulled by meths
Children scratch sores – sleep
bitten by the tsetse flies of Soweto
of June 16
(Noordgesig lies on the fringes of Soweto).

It is sleepy in the "coloured" townships.
A pensioner in Coronation
lies dead for a week
before the stench of her corpse
attracts attention through keyholes
and windows.

It is sleepy in the "coloured" townships.
A neighbour's son watches as silkworms

encrusted on mulberry leaves
wrap themselves into cocoons of silk.

It is sleepy in the "coloured" townships.
It is sleepy in Riverlea and Noordgesig
Eldorado's Park, Bosmont, Newclare
It is sleepy in all the "coloured" townships

CANDLE

for Caplan

Read brother read.
      The wax is melting fast
      The shadows become obdurate
      and mock pantomimes of you
      laughing through crude cement
      in silent stage whispers.

Read brother read,
      though the wax lies heaped
      in the saucer
      and the silhouettes of gloom
      grow longer.

Read brother read.
      Only the wick shines red now.
      But it is not yet dark.
      Remember brother,
      it is not yet dark.

I was hardly four and living at my granny's
when the news came
as it does to all four-year-olds
from the overhanging vines of the adults,
through the eaves of the wise who suddenly
are not so wise.
Cooking stopped.
Panic shattered the eardrum of the cup of peace.

All was not well,
not only two miles down the road
from where an out-of-breath boy
had brought the news
in short telegram gasps.

Quickly Granny wrapped me in a blanket as cold
as the flag of a sad country,
took me away to my mother
whose tears by now were warmer, had more salt
than the dead child, brother, grandchild.

Along the rough road, cobbled with the dirges of beer cans,
tremulous with stones and filled with more people
than children born to the world that day,
my grandmother walked, and for her the road grew shorter.
For me staring over her shoulder, longer and longer.

WE CAN'T MEET HERE, BROTHER

for Thami Mnyele

We can't meet here, brother.
We can't talk here in this cold stone world
where whites buy time on credit cards.

I can't hear you, brother!
for the noise of the theorists
and the clanging machinery of the liberal Press!

I want to smell the warmth of your friendship, Thami
Not the pollution of gunsmoke and white suicides.

We can't meet here, brother.
Let's go to your home
Where we can stroll in the underbrush of your paintings
Discuss colour
Hone assegais on the edges of serrated tongues.

✓

IN DETENTION

He fell from the ninth floor
He hanged himself
He slipped on a piece of soap while washing
He hanged himself
He slipped on a piece of soap while washing
He fell from the ninth floor
He hanged himself while washing
He slipped from the ninth floor
He hung from the ninth floor
He slipped on the ninth floor while washing
He fell from a piece of soap while slipping

140

He hung from the ninth floor
He washed from the ninth floor while slipping
He hung from a piece of soap while washing

A RIOT POLICEMAN

The sun has gone down
with the last doused flame.
Tonight's last bullet
has singed the day's last victim
an hour ago.
It is time to go home.

The hippo crawls
in a desultory air of triumph
through, around fluttering
shirts and shoes full of death.
Teargas is simmering.
Tears have been dried by heat
or cooled by death.
Buckshot fills the space
between the maimed and mourners.
It is time to go home.

A black man surrenders
a stolen bottle of brandy
scurries away with his life
in his hands.
The policeman rests the oasis
on his lips
wipes his mouth on a camouflaged
cuff.
It is time to go home.

141

Tonight he'll shed his uniform.
Put on his pyjamas.
Play with his children.
Make love to his wife.
Tomorrow is pay-day.
But it is time to go home now,
It is time to go home.

Peter Horn

THE ERUPTION OF LANGA, 30TH MARCH 1960

after Bertolt Brecht

I've been told that the streets were black
black lava which flowed
over a mile long from Langa
to Caledon Square Police station
and the flood spread at the foot of the mountain

Those who observed the phenomenon
from armoured cars and helicopters
reported
that all was well but their faces were ashen

Stephen Gray

LOCAL HISTORY

> In this hunched low seaside resort
> > crusted in leisure and dough
> (the riots continue elsewhere out of reach
> > the fishermen trawl for no fish)
> I sit and compose myself to write
>
> and as I sit and compose myself here
> > (the riots continue
> the fishermen fish out the end of the sea)
> > and as I compose and
> sit and write a history of local endeavour
>
> (the riots continue to flourish out there
> > there are no fish in the sea)
> cramped in leisure and fed up on dough
> > I sit and compose myself
> for the time when you burn like a shoal on me

SONG OF THE GOLD COMING IN

> Over a brutal landmass I hover
> at night like an ear of corn
> bending across your attraction
>
> many's the scalding circle
> I make around day and night
> always drawing in for you
>
> some say I'm aflame just for you
> I was always destined for you
> but many say that at me

I'm young enough to be choosy
I don't mind circuiting for ever
I'm untouchably beautiful

burning and rolling so slim
what a piece of tail you say
my light makes even you adorable

but now I'm helpless I fall
I'm raining fire I can't hold
I shall pock all your skin

I sink on your stomach
your chest on your teeth
I'm like sweat lightening you

o and I stroke you so hot
was there ever such a crashlanding
you're drawing me down take me

into your innermost cavern
bury me deep I'm ashamed
I'm broken I am no more

I belong to you now
I can feel your heart shift
I know I must love you now

but some say I was always yours
I never corroded stayed contrary
thrown out from your depths

I suppose you try and void me
belch me out in forges of lava
hurl me about like pus

but I lie in your armpits and groin
always resistant always me
as indigestible as a saint

and you dark cannibal whom I
love throw me out throw me
out from your burning guts

so I rest here for always
like a chain at your neck
or a warm sun on your earlobes

watching you guarding you
making you rich every moment
until you stop hating me.

Patrick Cullinan

TO HAVE LOVE

To have love and then lose it:
the white hail in the orchard
lying with leaves it has stripped
and the storm moving away.

THE FIRST, FAR BEAT

In the mountains
the first, far beat
of spring thunder:

thick with young,
a lizard on the rock
moves its head

and in the flank
the quick heart pulses.

THE DUST IN THE WIND

The grass black and a turbulence,
a blossoming
that shakes from the plum tree
clockwise,
that drops a hundred yards away.

Spring comes with its mortal odours,
a flicker of red in the hills at night,
and age is a taste, dry on the tongue
all day
there is dust in the wind.

This morning we moved North again
Through strange bush.
We know the enemy still follows:
By night we see their fires,
By day their dust.

The old men talk, still,
Of our ancestors from North:
About the rich forests
And swarming game,
And of our return
Which is ordained
In the stars.
I see no sign of this North.
There are smaller trees
And unknown roots, more snakes
And fewer birds.
On a long journey
The land must change.

I think they will cut us off tomorrow.
There was dust this evening
On our right flank. Is it because
They do not want to fight
Among the hills ahead?
Mountains were our country:
They fear ambush and they are right
There is no mercy between us:
They are so many.

On watch tonight I stare
At one point in the blank sky.
A star glitters. At once
It is there, as though my staring

Brought it out.
Was it ordained?
The star is in the South.

The women and the children sleep
In the warm heart of the camp.
It is not death I fear
But the thought that birth will stop.
I fear the end of my people.

SIR TOM

No longer seen at office or the club, he was "retired":
flailing around his Randlord house each day he'd
light his high Victorian lamps in every room
to search for mambas, or he'd plead

for "sweeties" from his own black cook, who shyly wept
to see his master so demeaned. He'd slaver
at his neighbor's fence and shout that there were diamonds
in his rockery. With children he was meant to have a

special kind of sympathy. I was his favorite,
so my parents said, and when we went to luncheon
once a month on Sunday, they'd place me on a high stool
next to "Father." He'd say grace, then punch upon

the table, shout "my sweet boy" and squeeze my puny chin
with his gross hand, while all around us aunts
and uncles kept on smiling: awkward, docile, prim, as course
would follow course, borne by servants

older than Igoli. They'd dodder on from place to place
with plates of sugared pumpkin, beans or yellow rice. All style,

all energy was broken in that room, the curtains drawn
against the post-noon sun. Talk would last a while

then hush down to a silent, sated calm, so all you'd hear
would be the clink of knife and fork against the plate
as close on twenty people waited till it took
the old man's wit to start again, to speak. It was my fate

that one such afternoon he turned to me and asked:
"What would you like, my darling boy?" Without thinking,
I said I wanted toast. So toast was brought. It came
on its own dish and in a silver rack. The old man winking

to the table – for all his children and their children
had paused and now were watching – took off the covering
napkin, drew out a piece and lavished it in butter,
nimbly slicing off the crusts. Hovering

behind us I heard Jim, the oldest servant there,
just barely whisper "shame," though why he said this I
did not understand quite then. A square of soft, warm
butter-sodden toast filled the middle of the plate. "Why,

close your eyes, my boy," the old man said, "Open
wide!" I made my lips into an O, smiling to the giver.
Eyes shut, I turned towards grandfather,
trusting. Into my throat he jabbed a long coarse sliver

from the crust. It rasped and burnt my skin. I gagged
in panic and could not scream while still he stabbed and bent
it down my throat. Some uncle (or my father, was it?)
pulled him gently off. Choked with shock, I was quickly sent

or carried from the dining room and put upon
a couch in the small parlour. At the table old Sir Tom
stared at his family. Rightly, they had always known
children never should presume or, if they did, learn that from

such babies must come men. But strangely, now, the old man
  broke,
gasping into tears. He said he saw white skulls and not
their cosy, smiling faces. Blue-eyed, haggard, he too was led
sobbing from the table. Perhaps, at last, he'd understood

how sick he was and old, hearing Doom's blatancy:
the awful nonsense raving, Hell seething in his head.

ETRUSCAN GIRL

It is a moving thing
to see in this figure
how the maker
has shown the girl
or young woman
plaiting her hair
so that the arm and fingers
as they move,
the tress itself,
are one piece in the clay,
fused, that no part
of the model should crack
in the oven,
that no part of the moment
be lost.

Just two foot high –
it might have been
an image for her tomb:
but who knows that
or anything
about this girl
who has no name,

no story? Even
the tongue she spoke
is blocked, obscure:
dust upon dust,
twenty-five centuries,
annulling
all memory.

And the figure half turns
to stare at me,
as though I
could give a name:
as though death did not
repeal identity,
as though there were
a body there,
a spirit that I must see,
clearly.

And I try to imagine
those who called
the craftsman in,
the maker,
saying to him:
You knew   , you knew her well,
make her for us, make her
as we knew her in this life.

And it was
as he had seen her last,
sitting outside the house,
debonair in the morning,
plaiting her hair in the sun,
the hands and fingers quickly
pushing in and out
so closely that

152

the moment and the movement
fused:
and the maker saw
that they were one.

In memoriam S. B. C.

Don Maclennan

In his old age my father
managed to make his writing
flow like water,
ripples across a paper lake
pierced with upright stakes.
I could read waves then,
so it was not hard to follow.
Now mine begins to look the same,
but the waves run off the page
mocking my inability
to contain my age.

My father's letters look
like frozen lakes,
stiff unyielding waves,
hungry cormorants
perched on frosty stakes –
words lock-jawed
waiting for the thaw.

Summer is outrageous:
northern swallows,
fields of waist-high grass,
a moon of burning sulphur
above the sandstone hills.

And writing?
Flinging words
against the world,
to conjure up the sound
and smell of things
that are themselves.

"WINTER SUNLIGHT, CLEAN AS A CUT ORANGE . . . "

Winter sunlight, clean as a cut orange.
A stone wall breaks the wind.
I came here throwing off weight,
up a dry river bed under acacia trees,
touching boulders of dolerite.

For over sixty years I have been lost,
and now renew myself by memory
of entrance from that other place
knowing this one was more desired.
What do I look for now?
Words warm in the brain that are
tree, water, stone.

So the smell of woodfires,
aromatic herbs, washed hair, flesh,
a scrubbed table, books, bread,
clean clothes, dryness of the midday air,
and the sun, like a cut orange,
spilling fragrance everywhere.

FUNERAL III

The metaphors the minister employed
were ancient seeds as edible as wheat:
whatever dies becomes the food
of new existence and outlives
death's appetite miraculously.

But the conversation of the pigeons on the roof
broke my willing suspension of disbelief.

Let the dead bury the dead.
I went out and bought hot bread,
took bread and tea
and ate it in the garden.
Eating in the sun
with flies and ants
seemed right.

Douglas Livingstone

GENTLING A WILDCAT

Not much wild life, roared Mine leonine Host
from the fringe of a forest of crackles
round an old dome-headed steam radio,
between hotel and river – a mile of bush –
except for the wildcats and jackals.

And he, of these parts for years, was right.
That evening I ventured with no trepidations
and a torch, towed by the faculty
I cannot understand, that has got me
into too many situations.

Under a tree, in filtered moonlight,
a ragged heap of dusty leaves stopped moving.
A cat lay there, open from chin to loins;
lower viscera missing; truncated tubes
and bitten-off things protruding.

Little blood there was, but a mess of
damaged lungs; straining to hold its breath
for quiet; claws fixed curved and jutting,
jammed open in a stench of jackal meat;
it tried to raise its head hating the mystery, death.

The big spade-skull with its lynx-fat cheeks
aggressive still, raging eyes hooked in me, game;
nostrils pulling at a tight mask of anger
and fear; then I remembered hearing
they are quite impossible to tame.

Closely, in a bowl of unmoving roots,
an untouched carcass, unlicked, swaddled and wrapped
in trappings of birth, the first of a litter stretched.

Rooted out in mid-confinement: a time
when jackals have courage enough for a wildcat.

In some things too, I am a coward,
and could not here punch down with braced thumb,
lift the nullifying stone or stiff-edged hand
to axe with mercy the nape of her spine.
Besides, I convinced myself, she was numb.

And oppressively, something felt wrong:
not her approaching melting with earth,
but in lifetimes of claws, kaleidoscopes:
moon-claws, sun-claws, teeth after death,
certainly both at mating and birth.

So I sat and gentled her with my hand,
not moving much but saying things, using my voice;
and she became gentle, affording herself
the influent luxury of breathing –
untrammelled, bubbly, safe in its noise.

Later, calmed, despite her tides of pain,
she let me ease her claws, the ends of the battle,
pulling off the trapped and rancid flesh.
Her miniature limbs of iron relaxed.
She died with hardly a rattle.

I placed her peaceful ungrinning corpse
and that of her firstborn in the topgallants
of a young tree, out of ground reach, to grow: restart
a cycle of maybe something more pastoral,
commencing with beetles, then maggots, then ants.

The blue duiker, left hindleg
in a poacher's noose held
to a piece of earth by an iron peg,
stands, heart jumping, puzzled;
his scared velvet ears spread
to the sly rustle of leaves and stems;
huge tired eyes probing
the recesses of his epoch's dusk.

He has been snared for three days
of sleepless terror; throat scorched with thirst,
tongue thick from rust, dust and blood,
one tiny horn broken from his first
fight with the iron in the earth's skin.
The footloose poacher, long gone
for weeks, has moved on,
will not be returning.

At lengthening intervals
the hare-sized buck gathers himself
for bounding, mouth wide and whistling,
to tow the piece of earth with him.
The wire bites tighter.
Blood flows, clots, runs, congeals
until metal wholly rings on bone.
The earth remains unmoving.

He stops aghast at his noise;
quivering, pants quietly;
resumes his frenzied leaping.
Soon, small herbivorous teeth
will have to grit to gnaw through pain.
Water lies a doubtful day
away: a three-legged stumble through
hyena-patrolled terrain.

Cold evenings: red tongues and shadows
spar under this dangerous thatch
rust-patched; one weather wall of planks;
long-limbed tools, wood, coal in smoke-dimmed stacks;
a hitched foal's harness musical.

The grindstone's rasped pyrotechnic
threatens the stopped-dead angled tip
of a stripped Cape cart that waits on
the return of its motivation;
a sudden hiss as quenched irons cool.

Two cowled purple-cheeked bellows-boys
pump, or jump for smiths or furies;
files of elders sucking pipestems,
ordered by fire's old feudalism,
squat: wrinkled jury on this skill.

Horseshoes, blades, shares and lives: all shaped
to the hoarse roar and crack of flame,
by the clang of metallic chords,
hammer-song, the anvil's undertone;
nailed to one post a jackal's skull.

Jeremy Cronin

"TO LEARN HOW TO SPEAK . . . "

To learn how to speak
With the voices of the land,
To parse the speech it its rivers,
To catch in the inarticulate grunt,
Stammer, call, cry, babble, tongue's knot
A sense of the stoneness of these stones
From which all words are cut.
To trace with the tongue wagon-trails
Saying the suffix of their aches in -kuil, -pan, -fontein,
In watery names that confirm
The dryness of their ways.
To visit the places of occlusion, or the lick
In a vlei-bank dawn.
To bury my mouth in the pit of your arm,
In that planetarium,
Pectoral beginning to the nub of time
Down there close to the water-table, to feel
The full moon as it drums
At the back of my throat
Its cow-skinned vowel.
To write a poem with words like:
I'm telling you,
Stompie, stickfast, golovan,
Songololo, just boombang, just
To understand the least inflections,
To voice without swallowing .
Syllables born in tin shacks, or catch
The 5.15 ikwata bust fife
Chwannisberg train, to reach
The low chant of the mine gang's
Mineral glow of our people's unbreakable resolve.

To learn how to speak
With the voices of this land.

Our land holds its hard
Wooden truths like a peach
A pip:
      Out at Athlone
By the power station
Over two cooling towers, the wind
Turns visible in its spoors.
Skin and bone, zig-zag,
Through the khaki bush
It hums, the wind tongues
Its gom-gom, frets a gorah,
In a gwarrie bush the wind,
So I fancy, mourns, thin
Thin with worries:
      Goringhaicona
Goringhaiqua Gorachouqua: sounds
Like at the back of our sky
Cicadas' songs ache: Hessequa
Hacumqua, like vocables swallowed
In frogs' throats: Cochoqua,
The names of decimated
Khoikhoin tribes – their cattle stolen,
Lands seized
As their warriors died
Charging zig-zag into musket fire,
Those warriors who've left behind
Their fallen spears that our land
Like a peach its pip
      Holds now:

This unfinished task.

Thoughts
    concerning the person
    named Who:
Who is naked beneath his clothes,
Who is black in the night,
Who is
    unwashed before his bath,
and you mustn't suck cents
    you never know
Who might have touched them last.
Who is mask.
Who is beyond
    mask, lock, yale, bolt, chain, electric alarm.
Who,
    son of Who,
Who's Who, when the dog barks
there also is Who.
Who peeps through windows.
Who desires my mother, without a pass.
Who wields
    a double-edged knife.
Who entertains
    my darkest
desires.
Who,
    a temporary permanent
sojourner in my dream's backyard.
Who walks through our night.
Who stalks our women.
Who looks at my sister
    with longing.
      Yes,
Who.

For a body I've rolled up
inventory item six two three: one pair
socks short prisoner's European, dealt
for a tail
a tight hand from a scuffed
awaiting-trial playing card pack and added
50 finest quality
Rizla gummed
cigarette blaadjies scorched black.
From a prison cell floor comes this barred
light of your back, your
beak was bent
uptight for a week, your call with its
inner-side scratch I've rasped, your eyes
sharpened on the grindstone
down in the prison workshop, then dipped
in an old Koo tin of water from which they emerge
dripping light
nail sharp, tense, each as an i-dot.
I check your
hungry parts
over again, longing by longing then
out
over the high walls I launch you now . . .

      sshrike!

MOTHO KE MOTHO KA BATHO BABANG

A PERSON IS A PERSON BECAUSE OF OTHER
PEOPLE

By holding my mirror out of the window I see
Clear to the end of the passage.
There's a person down there.
A prisoner polishing a doorhandle.
In the mirror I see him see
My face in the mirror,
I see the fingertips of his free hand
Bunch together, as if to make
An object the size of a badge
Which travels up to his forehead
The place of an imaginary cap.
      (This means: *A warder.*)
Two fingers are extended in a vee
And wiggle like two antennae.
      (He's being watched.)
A finger of his free hand makes a watch-hand's arc
On the wrist of his polishing arm without
Disrupting the slow-slow rhythm of his work.
      (*Later*. Maybe, later we can speak.)
Hey! Wat maak jy daar?
      – a voice from around the corner.
No. Just polishing baas.
He turns his back to me, now watch
His free hand, the talkative one,
Slips quietly behind
      – *Strength brother*, it says,
In my mirror,
      A black fist.

Prologue

In the prison workshop, also known as the seminar room;

In the seminar room, sawdust up the nose, feet in plane shavings, old jam tins on racks, a dropped plank, planks, a stack of mason's floats waiting assembly, Warder von Loggerenberg sitting in the corner;

In the prison workshop, also and otherwise named, where work is done by enforced dosage, between political discussion, theoretical discussion, tactical discussion, bemoaning of life without women, sawdust up the nose, while raging at bench 4, for a week long, a discussion raging, above the hum of the exhaust fans, on how to distinguish the concept "Productive" from the concept . . . "Unproductive Labour";

In the prison workshop, then, over the months, over the screech of the grindstone, I'm asking John Matthews about his life and times, as I crank the handle, he's sharpening a plane blade, holding it up in the light to check on its bevel, dipping the blade to cool in a tin of water, then back to the grindstone, sparks fly: "I work for myself" – he says – "not for the boere";

In the prison workshop, with John Matthews making contraband goeters, boxes, ashtrays, smokkel salt cellars of, oh, delicate dove-tailings;

Over the months, then, in the prison workshop, I'm asking John Matthews, while he works intently, he likes manual work, he likes the feel of woodgrain, he doesn't like talking too much, the making and fixing of things he likes, he likes, agh no, hayikona, slap-bang-bang, work for the jailers;

In the prison workshop, then, I ask John Matthews, was he present
on the two days of Kliptown . . . 1955? . . . when the People's
Congress adopted the Freedom Charter?

Actually

No he wasn't

He was there the day before, he built the platform

In the prison workshop, then, over the hum of exhaust fans, between
the knocking in of nails, the concept "Productive," the concept
"Unproductive Labour," feet in plane shavings, John Matthews
speaks by snatches, the making and fixing of things he likes,
though much, never, much you won't catch him speaking;

But here, pieced together, here from many months, from the prison
workshop

Here is one comrade's story.

                    *

Born to Bez Valley, Joburg
into the last of his jail term
stooped now he has grown

In this undernourished frame
that dates back
to those first years of his life.

He was nine
when his father came
blacklisted home

From the 1922
Rand Revolt,
and there with a makeshift

Forge in their backyard
a never again to be employed
father passed on to his son

A lifelong
love for the making
and fixing of things.

From Bez Valley it was,
veiled like a bride in fine
mine-dump dust

He went out
to whom it may concern
comma

A dependable lad
comma
his spelling is good.

At fifteen he became
office boy at Katzenellenbogen's
cnr. von Wielligh

And President streets
where he earned: £1 a week,
where he learned:

* Good spelling doesn't always count.
* The GPO telegram charge is reckoned per word.
* A word is 15 letters max.
* You have to drop ONE / from Katzenellen-
   bogen Inc or

HEAR ME BOY?! nex' time
YOU'S gonna pay extra one word
charge your bliksem self.

And the recession came
but he got a bookkeeping job
with Kobe Silk

On the same block
        – John Edward
Matthews

Mondays to Fridays
on that same block
for 37 unbroken years until

The security police
picked him up . . . . But first
way back to the thirties.

WEEKENDS IN THE THIRTIES:
church and picnics
by Zoo Lake.

And later, deedle-deedle
– Dulcie, heel-toe,
his future wife

Whom he courted with
(he can still do it)
diddle-diddle: the cake-walk

And always
on Sundays it was
church and church.

And then to Kobe Silk
there came
a new clerk

Myer Chames by name
a short little bugger who talked
Economics at lunch-break

And Myer Chames talked
of all hitherto existing societies,
the history of freeman

And slave, lord, serf,
guildmaster, journeyman,
bourgeois, proletarian and

In a word
John Matthews stopped
going to church.

His name got inscribed
inside
of a red party card.

He'd sell Inkululekos down by
Jeppestown
Friday nights

While the bourgeois press wrote
    RUSSIA HAS GONE SOFT ON HITLER
He learnt to fix duplicators and typewriters.

He was still selling
Inkululekos in 1943
when even the bourgeois press wrote

RED ARMY HAS BROKEN
BROKEN
THE BACK OF HITLER

In the year 1943 – born
to Dulcie and John
a daughter

Their first child
first of seven.
And now

Into the last months
of his 15 years
prison term

At nights in his cell
he peeps down at his face
in a mirror

In a mirror held low, about
belly-height,
wondering how he'll seem

To his grandchildren
from down there
next year when he comes out.

But that's later . . . back
to 1950
The Suppression of Communism Act

Membership becomes a punishable crime
But laws only
postpone matters – somewhat.

There were still duplicators to fix
and typewriters to mend
through the 50s

Passive Resistance, the Congress Alliance, Defiance Campaign, Pass
    Burnings, Bus Boycott, Potato Boycott, the Women's March, the
    Treason Trial, the Freedom Charter, until

Until 1960: the massacre
        Sharpeville
        and Langa.

And people said: "Enough,
        our patience, it has limits" . . . and so
it was no longer just typewriters and duplicators to mend.

A man would come to the backyard and whisper: 30 ignitors.
And John Matthews would make 30, to be delivered to X.
And a man would come in the dead of night
These need storing comrade, some things wrapped in waterproof
    cloth.
        TERRORISTS BOMB POWERLINES
He would read in the bourgeois press, or
        MIDNIGHT PASS OFFICE BLAST
He'd sigh a small sigh
 – Hadn't been sure
Those damned ignitors would work.

Finally.
1964.
After a quarter century in the struggle

A security police swoop
and John Matthews was one
among several detained.

White and 52
so they treated him nice.
They only made him stand

On two bricks
for three days
and three nights and

When he asked to go to the lavatory
they said:
          Shit in your pants.

But the State needed witnesses
So they changed their tune.
Tried sweet-talking him round.
Think of your career
          (that didn't work)
Think of the shame of going to jail
          (that thought only
          filled him with pride)
You really want kaffirs to rule?
          (like you said)
Think of your wife
          (Dulcie. Dulcie.
          7 kids. Dulcie.
          She's not political at all).

And there they had him.
On that score he was worried, it's true.
And they promised him freedom.
And they pressed him for weeks on end
Until finally he said:

Okay, agreed.

– But first I must speak with my wife.

Barely an hour it took them to find
and rush Dulcie Matthews
out to Pretoria Jail.

Then looking nice, because they let him shave, let him comb his hair,
    looking nice then, chaperoned by smiling, matrimonial policemen,
    shaven and combed, John Matthews got led out to his wife, and
    holding her hand, they let him hold her hand, he said
– Do you know why they've brought you?
And she said
– I do.
And he said
– Dulcie, I will never betray my comrades.
And with a frog in her throat she replied
– I'm behind you. One hundred percent.

So back they hauled John Matthews then and there,
back to the cells,
that was that, then, but
all the way down the passage
toe-heel, heel-toe, diddle-diddle
ONE HUNDRED PERCENT
I mean, he was high
off the ground, man.

He was walking on air.

I SAW YOUR MOTHER

I saw your mother
with two guards
through a glass plate
for one quarter hour
on the day that you died.

"Extra visit, special favour"
I was told, and warned
"The visit will be stopped
if politics is discussed.
Verstaan – understand!?"
on the day that you died.

I couldn't place
my arm around her,
around your mother
when she sobbed.

Fifteen minutes up
I was led
back to the workshop.
Your death, my wife,
one crime they managed
not to perpetrate
on the day that you died.

YOUR DEEP HAIR

Remember the mierkat's
footfall down the inner-sleeve of night,
under the milkbush, under the curdled
star clouds of galactic semen
spilled across the sky, you turned in sleep and
from your deep hair tumbled
aromatic buchu and the wide veld.

Three months now.
Scalp shaved,
you died, they say,
your head encased in wraps.

Gcina Mhlophe

THE DANCER

Mama,
they tell me you were a dancer
they tell me you had long beautiful legs
to carry your graceful body
they tell me you were a dancer

Mama,
they tell me you sang beautiful solos
they tell me you closed your eyes
always when the feeling of the song
was right, and lifted your face up to the sky
they tell me you were an enchanting dancer

Mama,
they tell me you were always so gentle
they talk of a willow tree
swaying lovingly over clear running water
in early spring when they talk of you
they tell me you were a slow dancer

Mama,
they tell me you were a wedding dancer!
they tell me you smiled and closed your eyes
your arms curving outward just a little
and your feet shuffling in the sand;
tshi tshi tshitshitshi tha, tshitshi tshitshitshi tha . . .
O hee! how I wish I was there to see you
they tell me you were a pleasure to watch

Mama,
they tell me I am a dancer too
but I don't know . . .
I don't know for sure what a wedding dancer is
there are so many funerals

where we sing and dance
running fast with the coffin
of a would-be bride or a would-be groom
strange smiles have replaced our tears
our eyes are full of vengeance, Mama

Dear, dear Mama,
they tell me I am a funeral dancer.

THE BODY IS A COUNTRY OF JOY AND PAIN

A Door to the Soul

If it was a dream, then it was dreamed each week
in a waking sleep, a woman seeing her children
running in a cloud of cries and expectations
along a corridor towards her until the moment
just before they would reach her waiting arms
and a hidden guard would release an iron door
that would fall with a crash between them,
and the children would run headlong into it,
and she would hear their small hands beating
once, twice against it as they dragged her away
and back to the cell, where they would watch her,
hour after hour, sitting and weeping, beating
her own arms until they ached, imagining them
filled to overflowing with noise and bustle.

One Sunday in November

They removed all of his days and left him with
hours. Then they removed all of his hours
and left him with minutes. Then they removed
all of his minutes and left him with a silence
that had no line or horizon, and time vanished
into the walls around him. After two years
they gave him one day of faces and voices,
words and the touching of hands and of lips.
And then once more they left him with the hard
pebble his fingers had held and worn smooth.
And when no one was left who remembered him,
they left him alone to blink through his tears
at the searing brightness of sunlight as he
stood in an empty street filled with people.

A Flight of Birds

One after the other they entered the room
and forced open her legs, grunting and sweating,
slamming into her, slamming, one after the other,
unbuttoning and unzipping, forcing into her,
one after the other, turning her over and forcing
into her as she screamed, the pain and fear
blurring, without stopping, all night and all
of the following day, the room filled with blows
and laughter, the smells of tobacco and alcohol.
And years later, sitting in her kitchen, she
lays down her knife and fork, and her shoulders
shake as she begins to weep, and the small hands
of her child fly out like birds through the air
to console her, but she cannot stop, and is gone.

The Question of Ownership

For the promise of his body, he said, he would
tell them anything they wished to know.
But slowly and methodically, piece by piece, they
removed it from him. And when they had finished
he could no longer recognise the penis that he
held each morning to urinate, nor the toes that
entered sock and shoe when he dressed in the morning,
nor even the rough feel of hands that trembled
as he raised a cigarette to his lips and drew smoke in.
It seemed as if his life belonged to another.
And for eight years he would search everywhere
and not find it, and would go on living
as someone else, someone who walked with a limp
and who was deaf, and who could not speak.

LAW AND ORDER

Rulers who neither see, nor feel, nor know,
But leech-like to their fainting country cling,
Till they drop, blind in blood, without a blow, –
A people starved and stabbed in the untilled field

There is a great commotion. Men and women
Run back and forth, in every direction, shouting,
"Who is the enemy? Where are they? What are they
Doing?" It is summer. There are days of flooding
And days of pain, and days of exaltation.
Warmth and possibility are strongly in the air.

And the men and the women who dress in long robes
And speak in the language of life and of death
Sit in solemn rows of doing and undoing. Their lips
Move, and their hands also, yet nothing happens.
Cracks open in the walls to let light in,
But their eyes cannot see it yet.

Elsewhere, it is the same as it was before.
A mother leaves in the darkness before dawn
To work all day, and for far too little.
A man stands alone in a forest of hands,
And is not seen, and only his hunger tells him
He is real, and must go on breathing out and in.

The body of a child only six years old
Becomes the body of a child only three years old.
And the body of a child only three years old
Becomes the body that we have before the world
Is houses and trees, fingers and years.
In this, there is no miracle. It happens every day.

In an emptied harbour, the last ship rocks
In water trembling with waves of expectation.
On deck, captains rush back and forth, in every direction,
Pointing and yelling, "Here he is. There they are.
She's the one. That's them. There, over there."
And purple veins stand out on their temples.

Elsewhere, in the high land that lies beyond
The line of mountains, the heat increases
And the short, green stalks turn into wheat.
Everyone sits through the long afternoons
On a verandah, half in sleep and half out,
Dreaming of death and the darkness to be reaped.

The grass dries and turns the colour of sand,
Grapes ripen and burst and seeds fall to the earth;
All around, the small creatures gather and eat.
Everything melts, and from the ocean a wind
Comes hurrying to rub out people and trees.
Inside the narrow kitchen of a lone house

A radio whines and crackles and loses the station,
And only the long sounds of distance remain.
Startled, the listeners look up and ask, "What
Is it? What has happened? Where are we?"
They walk in circles, making gestures and signs,
Seeing only themselves and the room they are in.

Elsewhere, a man walks into an empty field
And raises his arm, and does not return.
A woman sighs as she feels the delicate bones
Of her wrist dissolve beneath the weight
Of a blow that falls without mercy from behind.
A child out walking stumbles and falls

As a bullet glances from a wall and enters her chest.
In pain, she cries out for her father, but he
Does not hear, and she does not rise again.
All around, the cameras blink and remember,
While the men and the women who dress in long robes
And speak in the language of life and of death

Are startled from sleep, sit up and wonder,
"Is this it? Is it now done? Is this the end?"
It is summer. There are days of flooding
And days of pain, and days of exultation.
Warmth and possibility are solidly in the air,
Unstoppable brightness to come.

Donald Parenzee

THE RAINING

The raining
decades of war
have not stopped;

they fire
through windows now;
the eyes of millions shattered, light
soaks the earth
                        of a continent

Logically the storms flow
underground in streams.

African dreams,
liquid and thirsty.

INTERVIEW

for Megan, at ten years

At his home in the brilliant area,
casually slung between the parked cars
vacant on the peaceful driveway,
I pacify my indecision, stride

forward, press the bell; the room
invites like a lounge, another future
colleague who will also live like this
after the first red flush of discomfort.

The quiet, efficient public servant
tactfully takes my coat, my brief life

spreads its soft cloth
on the carpet: qualifications,

salary scales, fringe benefits;
ghostly pleats, tucks and hems
are planned for a new voice
in the college body politic.

Only to listen, perform a little snap
handshake and back out
into the warm suburban sun
scratching my itchy ignition finger

and be shaking again with the honest ecstasy
of our city's natural beauty,
spreading my weekend pleasures
guiltily through the week.

But your arms, as subtle as paper chains, fall
in the minutes before you leave
into sleep, lightly from my shoulders,
trusting that I shall never run, never desert to freedom.

And this interviewer, his childsface
distorted with horrific, secret lust,
I shall repay with portraits
of truths in children's minds.

CHANGES AT THE SETTLEMENT

The road is lifting at its gutters.
The front door dances like a broken leg.
In the kitchen the stubborn father
grabs at his glass,
hoping to still the precious water.

But these are not acts of God! he thinks
as each pebble falls.

Later the front end loader
bites off the northwest corner
and backs off clutching a piece
of the kitchen-dresser.

Certain things are too old
to carry around forever, anyway.

My friend had this black-and-white
news photograph
showing my mother's mother
in a most undignified pose:
lounge furniture all around her,
Table Mountain in the background.

I said, no thank you, those
memories I can do without

but now I'm not so sure.

Andries Walter Oliphant

CHILDHOOD IN HEIDELBERG

I was born in a house where ancestors
were suspended from the walls.
On hot afternoons
they would descend and walk silently
through the cool passages
of the dark house, slowly
as if strolling through a womb.

The roof is a vantage point for birds and pigeons.
On the stoep
in an ancient folding chair my namesake sits.
There is a giant gumtree
at the gate in which the sun sets.
The stars are candles
which my grandmother has lit.

Every morning father wakes to find a man
with a hole in his head
sleeping in the driftsand
of the furrow which runs
along the creosoted split-pole fence.
I go in search of the orchestra of crickets.

In the kitchen mother cries as she turns
the toast on the black plates
of the Welcome Dover.
When father packed my pigeons into boxes,
I ended up with Rover and the cats
on the back of a truck
with all the household goods.
I thought, if this is part of life, it's fun.

At the end of the truck's journey
through the sky, we arrived

in a toy town of match-box houses,
lined up like tombstones in a graveyard.
At once, I understood why my mother cried.

POEM FOR MY MOTHER

How far north and away from home
can one stray?
The northern light frays at the seams
so that I can see you across the distance:
out in the yard under blue heavens
hanging washing on a precarious line.

Between wooden poles and along
rusted wire fencing
the bright colours of my childhood
crack like so many flying flags.
I run in from the streets
to help you fold the linen when the day is dry.
First, our fingers touch,
then we walk away backwards
with the sheet stretched out
like a wide band of light between us.
Then we walk back to each other
to fold the sheet in half.
Before I go back I can see the affection in your eyes
When finally you have the pile
like the bound pages of a story book
against your chest,
I run back into the shadowed streets.

Before night-fall I do my all-important chores
of chopping wood
and filling a bucket with coal nuggets.

Before sunrise you are the only moving being
in a breathing house.
By the time the sun bursts upon the scene
you wipe perspiration from your face.
I greet you and go
into cold wet foreign streets.

Oregon, 1986.

AFTER LIFE

In memory of my father

In the month of your star
the sky teems
with barbels, carp, yellowtail and snoek.
On the banks of the Blesbok
you cast a line.
I cast a line at Dwesa from the rocks.
I see the split cane and the conoflex bend.

Late afternoon my car drones
through the rain.
I drive through the city
with the image of your catch
and our laughter
to the fire in your bed.

The gown they dressed you in
mimics the colours
of my infancy: yellow, blue and red
rectangles on a birthday shirt.
Your hands with which you speak
refer to udders round with milk.

And the truck you drove laden with pumpkins,
tomatoes, carrots, beetroot
and the fruit that kept me out
of other people's orchards.
When your land was taken
your right to live was confiscated.

How far did you cycle through that night?
With brown bread and pilchards
you kept us all alive.
While I made wire cars
with fish tails
which nobody would buy.

I came with a booth full of memories
swimming through my head like fish.
The rain was at the window
beating out a message which I could not read.
You said it was your mother, the midwife
and left me with your taciturn hat and pipe.

SONG OF THE UNEMPLOYED

This room with its brooding coal stove
And aluminium pots, unnerves me.
The broom standing in the corner.
And the black coat hanging from the wall.
What's in the cupboard below the window?

I stand in the doorway or look from the window
And see a grey dustbin
At the hingeless gate.
An aloe with spear-shaped leaves
Catches my eye:
What does it want to say?

191

Later today, I will take a plastic bucket
And fetch water
From a tap down the street.
I will step around puddles.
And avoid hungry-looking dogs.
Where do all the emaciated animals come from?

At dusk, when the first trains pull up,
I will stoke the fire,
Cook a huge pot of porridge,
Some vegetables
And a small portions of meat. Then
I will wait for my wife and children to return from work

THE HUNGER STRIKER

I hear my voice like the sombre rattle
of a diviner's bones:
After a life of eating porridge
with my hands from a dixie
I dream of waking up at home.

I sit at a table with a knife and fork.
The earth's edible crust
steaming in my porcelain plate.
I drink the sky distilled from a glass.
There is happiness the size of freedom in my cup.

But then I hear the stout voices of men in shorts
washing tin plates up.
The house in which I left a wife and child
is now deserted
and infested with rats and mice.

I go into the street and come across myself
shackled in leg irons
digging a hole in the sidewalk
big enough to hold my shrinking body.
The spade I was given has become an axe.

The baker from my childhood is in his doorway
with flour on his hands.
He speaks and I see
roasted corn spill from his mouth
like a praise poem to labour and productivity.

A girl passes on a bike and waves at me.
It looks like my daughter
in the clothes of my wife.
I cannot free my hands from the axe to wave back
I try to raise my leg but the irons restrain me.

My neighbour passes in an empty bus.
Through a broken window
he shouts at me:
The earth is full of yellow bones
which you must dig up.

I laugh like one immersed in life's conviviality
amid table cloths and serviettes.
Amid the repertoire of knives and forks,
the bright taste of pain
strikes me like a sharpened axe.

BLUE

There's blueness in the bush.
It rises from your chest,
your sweater and your vest.

193

It bursts from your pants
and from the sand
between your sunned legs.

I see the blueness
of the light
that plays about your mouth.

My love,
I drink the sky
from your perfect head.

Ingrid de Kok

SMALL PASSING

For a woman whose baby died stillborn, and who was told by a man to stop mourning, "because the trials and horrors suffered daily by black women in this country are more significant than the loss of one white child."

1

In this country you may not
suffer the death of your stillborn,
remember the last push into shadow and silence,
the useless wires and chords on your stomach,
the nurse's face, the walls, the afterbirth in a basin.
Do not touch your breasts
still full of purpose.
Do not circle the house,
pack, unpack the small clothes.
Do not lie awake at night hearing
the doctor say "It was just as well"
and "You can have another."
In this country you may not
mourn small passings.

See: the newspaper boy in the rain
will sleep tonight in a doorway.
The woman in the busline
may next month be on a train
to a place not her own.
The baby in the backyard now
will be sent to a tired aunt,
grow chubby, then lean,
return a stranger.
Mandela's daughter tried to find her father
through the glass. She thought they'd let her touch him.

And this woman's hands are so heavy when she dusts
the photographs of other children

they fall to the floor and break.
Clumsy woman, she moves so slowly
as if in a funeral rite.

On the pavements the nannies meet.
These are legal gatherings.
They talk about everything, about home,
while the children play among them,
their skins like litmus, their bonnets clean.

2

Small wrist in the grave.
Baby no one carried live
between houses, among trees.
Child shot running,
stones in his pocket,
boy's swollen stomach
full of hungry air.
Girls carrying babies
now much smaller than themselves.
Erosion. Soil washed down to sea.

3

I think these mothers dream
headstones of the unborn.
Their mourning rises like a wall
no vine will cling to.
They will not tell you your suffering is white.
They will not say it is just as well.
They will not compete for the ashes of infants
I think they may say to you:

Come with us to the place of mothers.
We will stroke your flat empty belly,
let you weep with us in the dark,

and arm you with one of our babies
to carry home on your back.

OUR SHARPEVILLE

I was playing hopscotch on the slate
when miners roared past in lorries,
their arms raised, signals at a crossing,
their chanting foreign and familiar,
like the call and answer of road gangs
across the veld, building hot arteries
from the heart of the Transvaal mine.

I ran to the gate to watch them pass.
And it seemed like a great caravan
moving across the desert to an oasis
I remembered from my Sunday school book:
olive trees, a deep jade pool,
men resting in clusters after a long journey,
the danger of the mission still around them,
and night falling, its silver stars just like the ones
you got for remembering your Bible texts.

Then my grandmother called from behind the front door,
her voice a stiff broom over the steps:
"Come inside; they do things to little girls."

For it was noon, and there was no jade pool.
Instead, a pool of blood that already had a living name
and grew like a shadow as the day lengthened.
The dead, buried in voices that reached even my gate,
the chanting men on the ambushed trucks,
these were not heroes in my town,
but maulers of children,

doing things that had to remain nameless.
And our Sharpeville was this fearful thing
that might tempt us across the wellswept streets.

If I had turned I would have seen
brocade curtains drawn tightly across sheer net ones,
known there were eyes behind both,
heard the dogs pacing in the locked yard next door.
But, walking backwards, all I felt was shame,
at being a girl, at having been found at the gate,
at having heard my grandmother lie
and at my fear her lie might be true.
Walking backwards, called back,
I returned to the closed rooms, home.

SUN, ALOE, RAIN

1

On the edge of scrub, where I grew up,
there were many veld fires in the brittle summer
and the heat in the heat consumed itself
and the air and land grew blacker and blacker.

I once saw a fire move like
coral lightning across the sand
after a meercat maddened
by the cremating arc.

And once, when the heat was like sandpaper, like scorpions,
I saw a salt pan under the high hard sun,
and watched the flamingoes rise, startled,
their underwings protected and pink.

In the veld were thorn trees in patches
like the dregs of other, imaginary gardens,
except in spring, when sticky with yellow life
they had another name, mimosa.

And in the gardens there were always aloes, sharp as blood,
and leathery cannas, all male flowers.
No one has yet put aloes and cannas
into a sweet-smelling basket or pitcher of water.

2

I remember going to a party,
seven and very severe,
in my sober dress two inches over my knee
and my high forehead and my mother's way.
There were lots of children
hiding and seeking, in shifting alliance,
while on the verandah the dog panted
and hopscotch lines simmered on the driveway.
I sat, more sullen than shy, licking my icecream carefully,
hating the aloes and cannas in their tended rows.

Playing games, no one noticed
the air was swelling, heavy on our heads,
and the ground sour with expectation.

Then the storm broke, an exploding rock,
a detonating jewel, its pieces of hot hail
knocking the cannas flat into the earth, puncturing aloes,
and the rain leapt over and over us.

When it was time to go, I ran
across the muddy grass, my back to an imagined breeze,
the yellow ribbons in my hair, loose and lovely,
breaking like waves against my long, thin neck.

1

Home is where the heart is:
a tin can tied to a stray dog.

The only truth is home truth:
preserves on the winter shelf.

Those who carry their homes on their backs
live for hundreds of years,
moving inch by inch from birth to lagoon.

2

Beside the beaten path
to the veld where I once played,
dry riverbed and unwashed clothes
grey lizards on the rocks.
My shadow squats in the shade of a thorn
where children sift and store
the remnants of corroded bins.
Over the path, the rocks, the tree,
marauding sky, fiercer than memory.

3

In a hot country
light is a leper,
water the eye of a goat
on the fork of an honoured guest.

The tap in the camp drips onto the bone of the gum.

And those in the cool green houses,
owners of the sweet white water,
owners of the bins and wells,
die swollen, host and guest of a herd of eyes
washing within them.

4

To return home, you have to drink its water,
in a drought, you have to drink its water,
even from the courtyard well,
the water blossoming in the gut,
or brackish, from a burning trough,
flypaper on your tongue,
pooling your hands,
bending when you drink.

5

Home is where the heart is:
husk of heat on the back.

The sky enters into the skin,
the sky's red ants
crawl over the shoulders.

This bending body is my only body.
I bend and drink
the shadow in the water.

THIS THING WE LEARN FROM OTHERS

From the hitchhiker whose head
falls against your shoulder in his sleep
as you swerve in the dark rain,
from two small boys waving
at a Safari Tour bus,
from others, that stowaway for instance,
who gave himself up because
from his hiding place
he couldn't smell the sea,
and from people who bury their dogs

in gardens, at night,
remembering the date until they are old.

They say if your mother held you
on her right side, head in the moist curve
of her arm, you are lonely,
and if she held you on her left,
her breast breathing into your ear,
you are lonely.

To be thus
is what we should have expected.

Only, at spring tide,
its moon just a glance
over the wet uncovered miles of sand,
the rocks white and black mica in the dark,
and waves which had buried themselves
at our feet, now trebling quietly
far out there
made us come close
to the fire on the beach,
made us think it possible
to stay that way,
scooping warm coals into the heart.

BRUSH STROKE

In the night a dream creases
you against me momentarily,
unfolding origami bird
in suspended rain, on a bending tree.

You brush beside me, the caress
guinea-fowl feathering my back.

Your dreaming leaves a ladder
leaning against a house of thatch.

You turn half in, half out of sleep
to lipread my dark silent mouth.
In our waking's slow ascent
I am the dream's aftertaste, its scent

INNER NOTE

Like a wishbone
or the instep of your foot

this parabolic love curves,
wings stirring

in the neck nerves of a crane
at marsh's edge,

or bends its back into a kite
arching the membrane of blue flight

You breathe me out
I breathe you in

the smell of your skin
is salt and tide and tin.

The half-open door
tilts cooler light

upon the floor
and outside sounds come in,

an olive thrush
through the hibiscus bush

last evening note
throating me under you.

This much is all we have:
shadows gathering,

fugitive grace,
and the deep body as our penumbral space.

GROUND WAVE

Just below the cottage door
our moraine stairway of lemon trees,
strelitzia quills and oleander shrub
steps to the sea and deeper terraces.
The warming wind, concertina on the slope,
coaxes open the bulbul's throat,
the figtree's testicular green globes
and camelia's white evening flux.

Behind the house we feel
the mountain's friction against our backs.
Deep fissures are predicted by the almanac,
earth and trees heaving to the shore.
Scorpions come in at night
for cool killings on the flagstone floor.

NORTH-WEST CAPE, 1985

Pale land, pale sky, where no snow melts the ironstone hills,
a cold wind is crossing eastwards to a salt, colder coast,
is cuffing yards of sand across the pallid, north-bound road.
A telephone wire dissects the sky, wind incised along its strand,
the trees are black, alarmed, as if electrocuted by past heat.
How much grief there is in rivers locked to their dry beds,
in waves breaking on a desert, the dunes blowing out to sea.
What grief will crowd these skies, all colour bled from them;
will, like volcanic peaks, rupture these heart-breaking plains.
Even now what bitterness is in the bushes, dry as old tobacco;
what bitterness in the camps of stone; and how much more today
in that man tramping, sockless, wind rifling his trouser-leg,
in that man seen labouring along the road, near nightfall, no
    house in sight,
forty-five kilometers from Steinkopf, forty-five to Vioolsdrif.

DESCENDING, LATE

for Peter Anderson

I

It will be dark, in cold, in stars,
stone bedded in the road like iron,
before you reach the final pass,
see far below the small farm lights.

The river beds itself in stone,
in night, as deeply as it can;
along this track, its road-bed sunk,
cold seeds itself in stone,

The cedars passing one by one
and black along the skylined peaks
that move with you as you move on
into the night that mountains make,

Beneath your soles a gravel's salt,
the juts of rock; against your skin
the charred fynbos a coral, dark,
far down this canyon's underworld:

A baboon barks, it almost screams:
the moon is up, over the Cedarberg,
and in the mountains to the east
the planet Mars is disappearing.

II

It will be more than late, long dark,
now this far off the stars convene,
the road more broken underfoot
as it drops through the shale-band.

You halt: far down the valley floor
a footfall rings, comes doubled back
into the emptiness you tread,
a strangeness self-estranging as

The cold in which the stars divide
in still more stars, the multiples
of stones that in this cold intrude
a stoniness against your bones –

Till you can't tell who it might be,
that sound of stone, or knock of boot;
if it was you, or one not you,
still moving down the night skyline,

A figure dark beneath its load,
hurrying through cold shades, the nek –
who halts again, the heavens wheeling,
to hear who moves, who halts.

III

You will be one become anoth-
er, moving down this final pass
in all the otherness of moon-
light, frost descending from the stars,

While moisture in the sand now crusts
in steep wind-boards of dirt and ice,
and there are two of you descend-
ing – there have long been two:

This one who walks, half-shivering,
another, ancient, watching him,
its face a shade, itself a stone,
but coming closer, alien, known

Beneath these stars and their star selves
that double in their cold descent
into the dark that mountains make,
against an earth that rules, divides

In its ironstone, these roads, the cry:
a sheep, its spasms, giving birth
close to that barbwired dry-stone wall,
in shadows black as frostbite.

Phil du Plessis

EASTER TRANSIT

Steinkopf 1983

The flanks
of these dire hills
bloom
wax-green.

Do they speak
of atonement,
of death,
of fragrant Spring
and blossom
on the hyssop,
do they speak
of another
Autumn?

On this journey
I go in the night,
into the night
while dry wind
escorts the moon
and me,
and roughens
the ridges.

Ahead on the road
the slaughterhouse truck:
and I
smell wool and dung and blood.

translated from the Afrikaans by Patrick Cullinan

Petra Müller

THREE SECTIONS FROM FORETELLING

for my mother – Anna Müller (died 1989)

gangrene

Mother dies from the fingertips backwards.
She is cold. She mewls; we hold her dark blue fingers
lightly in our hands. O what a clasp is there
in death: a wondrous woman known as lovely-Anne
in seven districts of the land. I slip the slippers
on her frozen feet and mumble to the sheepskinpile
that hugs her to the anklebone: come quickly,
fire-flesh. Have done.
For she was known for her complexion: little girls
came to her face to touch. O mother, cry. Do not forsake
your crying. For such a connoisseur as now comes by
to pay his homage to your loveliness
will take your blood's own flush into the dying clutch.
We are your daughters. And we watch.

palmiet to water

we are twined into a stream

living a reed's quiet life
I will eventually come to mother
the swirl of cycles
according to which you will always
pass me by, drawn
amber in the brown blood of my root,
the white foam of my riversong

what does the water think of
as it passes by?

– far away my mother rises as the leached breath
of the earth

she has left these playful flecked dreams behind
she is a clean white shower drifting towards peaks
she is rain
she gathers at the tips of leaves
soon her weight will draw down towards the
wooded earth
she is a small word spoken in an outer language
a single syllable

she has started on her limpid journey once again
when she passes by, I'll call her daughter

let it be yours

if there is to be a hand cupped
in eternity
to stave my fall

let it be yours
from which I fell

Antjie Krog

M A

Ma, I'm writing a poem for you
    without fancy punctuation
    without rhymes
    without adverbs
    just
    a barefoot poem –

because you raise me
in your small worn hands
you chisel me with your black eyes
and sharp words
you turn your slate head
you laugh and collapse my tents
but every night you offer me
to your Lord God.
your mole-marked ear is my only telephone
your house my only bible
your name my breakwater against life

mommy I'm so sorry
that I'm not
what I so much want to be for you.

translated from the Afrikaans by Karen Press

SONG OF THE CYCLISTS

five cyclists
five bolanders
from Salisbury to Malmesbury
        Riebeeckkasteel
the rustle of bicycle wheels
and the radiant sun on grandpa vests

strange as gypsies with a swartland burr
with skew mamre-caps
with rucksacks that cling like monkeys
 through Lupani
 through Jafuta
 Lundi
 across Matetsi

the fifth one
the brown one
the dreaming one   enmeshed in the clouds
arrived here long after the others
with beautiful feet and blue jeans
with Konakwa mountains right down his back
 Bamboesbaai
 Doringbaai
 Jacobsbaai
with piranhas in his black eyes
and an oar in his laugh

the brown one
the handsome one
I fell in love with him in a couple of hours
I lost him   also in a couple of hours
his shadow over his peugeot bicycle and dunlop tyres
over the mechanism   delicate as a web   as an alarm around
 jewels
his shadow unwinds in the distance
and I lose him

 even now . . .

translated from the Afrikaans by Karen Press

A ONE-DIMENSIONAL SONG FOR THE NORTHERN FREE STATE, MORE SPECIFICALLY MIDDENSPRUIT

most beloved state of heart estranged from spring
where maize crackles like stars
with rustblond beards distilling the moonlight
where sunflower fields spread handkerchiefs in the valleys
where clouds roll like horses
the late sun shoots out peacock feathers
across plump and broody fluff-green hills
each farm dam windmilled with willows
evening's last sparks fizzling
through heron-still waters

most beloved state of heart estranged from spring
where trains with ferns of smoke
go easily clicking and clucking each winter
over redgrass flecked with sparrow wings
over khakibush and blackjack echoing ironstone and guinea-fowl
reedbrown sandstonebrown dassiebrown winterbrown
white leghorn tufts in marshes
where partridges wobble like vetkoek at twilight
every winter morning cracks apart sharp as needles
a crisp willow-whip splits the frost
        the far-off puff of dung fires
        autumn feeding only on poplars
– power-lines chattering softly to each other

most beloved flat lands of my heart
where the jackknife of winter
casts itself completely
into the green harvest of summer
so many years I've tried to deaden our tie
and make your plains fertile in some other way
but each season I come to trace you again and again

for if I die this way I die
even in boland and bushveld
month in month out your redgrass blossom in my eyes.

translated from the Afrikaans by Denis Hirson

LOVESONG AFTER THE MUSIC OF K. E. NTSANE

"Feet, take me and carry me
carry me to the far side
she shines like an ostrichfeather
like a feather shines its shining vibration
soundlessly to the one who sits alone
alone under the willow she sits at ease."

(Mohlalefi stands that side of the river:
across the water he will come to me
for myself I choose not I was chosen
at the high gathering at Mokgatjane
a whirlwind gathers in the mountains
threads towards me like a needle through a hat)

"I greet you, Gray One with deep pools
you who cut across the farms of the whites
reptile who bites out dongas at the borders
when I want to cross you I am unsettled
I remember the days of the ancestors
when they fought for this land."

(Mohlalefi stands that side of the river:
across the water he will come to me
on the bank he stretches his legs
stretches his legs like a bird of prey
he rubs repeatedly at his chest
his heart rises like dough)

"Already I hear the tjhutjhumakgala
thing of the whites, millipede that clangs
that smokes pulling chains of smoke behind it
that wears a grass hat wrong side up
that thickens clear air, into the calm
it churns out cloud. It leaves us: pitchblack."

(Mohlalefi stands that side of the river:
across the water he will come to me
my body is charged my skin is light
every sinew glows like a filament
I anticipate your ears against my palms
my body will melt on your mats like butter)

"I greet you Moratuwa. I shall not
take you. Tilane moves his beard in the grave.
I will glide like a snake. I am bereft.
I am poor. The morninglight over Thaba Tseko
announces the pain of each day. Farewell Moratuwa,
I now become a warrior: Metsi a pshele re a bona:
            the water evaporates as we watch."

Translated from the Afrikaans by David Bunn, Jane Taylor, and the poet

'I DON'T GLANCE AT YOUR GRIZZLED HAIR

I don't glance at your grizzled hair
the tarnishing of fingers and teeth
first signs of plumpness at belly and rib
I hear only how your voice holds sway
a house around me keeping the elements at bay

I no longer glance at your fatigued eyes
but I watch your hands
weigh up child after child
and lay out our makeshift strategies

215

you endure me
you define me
you prop me on my feet
you fuse my explosive energies
sardonically weld masks for my chest

I make you
middle aged

oh hold me have me
overcome now kiss me
your moustache combing through my marrow
(not the man to master his woman
by way of some erotic web)
only tell me you take me
desire desire again
desire once again fire
my body till it seems I strangely vibrate
swell into my awkward defenceless breadwinner
uncork that fragrance careening and young
again be come we'll be again
all day all night long cock-full of fun

translated from the Afrikaans by Denis Hirson

TRANSPARENCY OF THE SOLE

the light over my desk
streams into darkness
I await my visitors on paper

my four children
finely balanced between anal and dorsal
tiny fins at the throat constantly stirring
eyes uncommonly soft

216

in the shallow brackish water your Mother treads clay
with metaphors

come here across dictionaries and blank pages
how I love this delicate little school
these fish of mine in their four-strong flotilla
lured so close now what should I feed you?

dear child of the lean flank
yield to the seabed
yes the stretching makes you
ache but Mother holds you to her your Mother
is here

the lower eye like Father's wondrous blue
migrates cautiously with a complex bunching
of nerve and muscle
till it's up beside the other
pert little mouth almost pulled out of shape
with time the tongue will settle in its groove
pigment of the upper flank beginning to darken

unobtrusive between sand and stone you lie
meshed with bedrock never
again to prey or take flight
I press my mouth against each distended face Mother knows

you will survive the tide

translated from the Afrikaans by Denis Hirson

REFUSED MARCH AT KROONSTAD MONDAY 23 OCT 1989

my thirty seventh year to heaven
I wake up in my town that I can only
   experience as backward in flat air-conditioned
     little shops jails with rose streamers
      fluttering fragrance
the house embraced by a scorching wind on this day
the day of my birthday while thousands
     start crowding close
    on the small greened square between town
and township: the march through my town today.

   ten I asked for. perhaps we'll find ten
ten whites that want to see the town reconciled the way it
   wants to spread its own freedom over cool
    banks. crickets carve the midday
    bare and willows smell
like bark. for the sake of ten of eight don't be angry
for the sake of five, alright then, of three for the sake
   of three don't destroy
    the town. sulphur and fire
hold back so that we can occupy it over again, new.

   roses gasp salmon-tongued from their buds at tea delicate
sandwiches light murmuring of peace
   spoilt gifts heartfelt wishes
    I know the march should now be heading to the left
    as far as the main street
here I sit with everthing white – thus I fail completely. my tongue
   too thin
my writing too gasping my language uncertain
   in hand and flees
    to paper. purblind town and all that burns
is my fist beside my own salt pillar of fear.

translated from the Afrikaans by Karen Press

218

under orders from my ancestors you were occupied
had I language I could write for you were land my land

but me you never wanted
no matter how I stretched to lie down
in rustling blue gums
in cattle lowering horns into Diepvlei
ripping the quivering jowls drink
in silky tassels in dripping gum
in thorn trees that have slid down into emptiness

me you never wanted
me you could never endure
time and again you shook me off
you rolled me out
land, slowly I became nameless in my mouth

now you are fought over
negotiated divided paddocked sold stolen mortgaged
I want to go underground with you land
land that would not have me
land that never belonged to me

land that I love more fruitlessly than before

translated from the Afrikaans by Karen Press

DISPOSSESSED WORDS

found poem

for Jessie Tamboer, who set herself alight and burned to death because she could no longer provide food for her children

> Trucks carried 40 000 blacks to the southern edge of the desert.
> I cannot say anything about my future now.
> > We had a very beautiful view
> > and this was the first time I saw my father cry
>
> They said "Old man, are you moving?"
> I took a crowbar, pulled the house down.
> I cannot say anything about my future now.

*

> > A man must have a dumping ground.
> > Every rabbit has got a warren.
> > A native must have a warren too.

*

> Sometimes I cry, I
> the absolute poor
> I am sick to death of watching my ruin.

*

> We had a very beautiful view of the sea –
> > This was refused.

*

Uncovering rubbish bins, I ask, could it not be that
something has been thrown in here – just a little
something that I can chew?

This was refused.

*

At times she would just suddenly start sobbing
without any apparent reason.

The absence of love.
There is no way you can describe that hunger.
Shining clean pots and jars:
There was no food whatsoever in the house.

*

She was immediately engulfed by flames but did not
utter a sound as she walked around the yard burning.

The ashes of one household are collected by another
for the bits of coal.
If you want to survive you must make a plan.

I cannot say anything about my future now.

*

*This poem is made out of words extracted from interviews with
people living in conditions of extreme poverty. The interviews
were conducted by researchers involved in the Second Carnegie
Inquiry into Poverty in South Africa.*

TIKOLOSH

"It was the tikolosh
who killed my child, the tikolosh did it,"
she was quite adamant. "I saw it."
They showed her the bullet holes,
they found the spent cartridge and showed her that,
but everything was simply further proof to her.
"Yes, I even saw the gun. The tikolosh carried a big gun."

She liked the idea of legal action.
"That will frighten the evil spirits," she said,
"though it will not bring back my poor child."
The policeman in the dock was embarrassed
when she kept calling him a tikolosh.
Eventually he burst out, "It was me,
you old fool, not some kaffir spirit.
It was me, with the gun, I know how to shoot!"

When they led him away she insisted on going up to him,
she touched his hand, he was forced to look at her,
and she said, "You poor creature, you do not know
what spirit haunts you."

In his cell he wept for a long time,
because it was true.

STATUES

Some lonely men stand around this city
petrified in difficult moments.

They have the eyes of people who never felt love,
so alone, achieving the country.

The people they achieved never notice them,
the contradictory pulling of muscles inside the metal.

Like stray outcroppings of rock.
It's impossible to believe they were ever the cause of anything

HEART'S HUNGER

I

I stored you against my eyelids
my treasure, more precious than water.

> *Then they stole my home, my land,*
> *the possibility of my hands, my last dress.*

I saw them, and when my eyes closed
I could not remember you.

> *Hunger has eaten my dreams.*
> *You are a scarecrow in a field*
> *the birds have plundered – useless love.*
> *Send money; I cannot eat your pink words.*

The moon will not believe me.
She says my heart is beating in your vanished hands.

II

This woman walking along the road
keeps seeing her heart fall behind her
bleeding into the buried caul.

This woman walking along the road keeps walking.

Her heart keeps falling away from her.

She roasts the falling heart on tinder fires
to sell to hungry travellers.

She dreams of arms wrapped around arms.

She dreams she is a feather on a flying bird.

She dreams of an enormous mother beckoning her.

She carries her father on her journey's back.

Her stomach is filled with his bones.

She bursts with pain and continues walking.

Her heart drops away, drops away.

She calls "I love you" in the wind.

The words hang like dead birds around her ears.

She is a stick no-one will hold.

    Far away, her name has faded on a man's dry skin.

She lies down on the gravel.

A thorn tree grows through her, pushing her upright.

III

The woman with the thorn tree growing through her chest arrives
   in the city.
She sees a picture of a house with grass and water,
and a doorway in which people embrace.
She decides to become such a house.

She sits on the sandy floor of the city.

She plucks an orange from the gutter and sells it to a hungry man

> A man grabs the orange and eats it fast,
> thinking the taste of the woman seller.
> It wasn't enough.

She has six cents in her hand, she shows it to the moon.

IV

The moon curses me, turning away
and I juggle with oranges in the dirt.
I juggle with coins I plaster my skin with hands.
The moon curses me, returning.

Everyone is hungry, every mouth eats me.
I am only so many crumbs of air, a sky
covered with ants, they carry me piece by piece away.
The moon stays, stroking the black bone beneath.

What if I had waited for him on the road?
Moon, you know nothing.
My hands held no offering for him.
I am cursed with myself.

V

Trader in hungers,
She grew strong.

And everything that could be eaten, was eaten.

She was bricks, words, skin, bread.

She was fire, milk, the road, the shade.

Her roof stretched wide across the city.

In her doorway, people embraced.

The moon grew thinner and thinner
watching over the wastelands of the country.

VI

Ghost against trees, lucent hunger
or thirst? Is it silver water
that would bring you back to me?

I am dry sticks, my love,
and I hunger so for the greenness
of hands on me, I am the carcass of dreams,
you may drift through my spaces.

Where do you sleep,
who do you love,
are you somewhere else a man?
Transparent love, your body
holds my earth and sky,
you are the window open on my drought.

You are a dead ghost.
I am rich and you will eat none of my coins.
You are a memory ghost.
Nothing is promised me,
from hunger to wealth I have come
through the desert of my heart.

NEEDLEWORK

From my needle small birds fly:
pink lattice feathers, leafgreen eyes,
yellow crests, plum spikes for tails.

Beside me on the metal pole
tubing threads down from a plastic bag
as thick and soft as a pound of liver:

your blood, midnight red stitches
of the deep needle filling you;
mine chainstitching bright birds.

THE FIRST THIRTY-SEVEN YEARS

We were just camping out
I put up a wall
and my mother bought carpets.
There was a door for the sea.

My father stood dropping anchor
year by year. I watched him lowering the rope,
he was swaying with a faraway look
and he said he loved me, lowering the rope.

My brother kicked a ball around a lot
and I was reading. I never knew
he broke his heart young.
I buried mine in a wave.

My father died. My mother went home.
My brother was away somewhere, walking.

I moved to the other side of the wall,
just camping out.

The sea could come in my sleep, or the wind.
I've no rope, my father left no rope.

CAN'T STAND, CAN'T DANCE

No-one's nailed down properly here.
There's always a corner loose and we wobble
bending over to hold it down.
There are these things down there –
id, morals, a national heart, keys –
sifting and circling as insistent gusts
lift that corner all the time. Other things blow in
and we have to keep checking
what's going on underneath
but we can't go all the way down
because
the other foot's hammered down fiercely over stones
that we own with grimacing pride,
determined proprietors of our birthright.
We're these cramped goblins hobbled to our accumulated selves,
holding up fistfuls of soil for balance:
can't stand, can't dance,
can't take a chance on an arabesque
in the space rolling past our borders.

FROM TIRESIAS IN THE CITY OF HEROES

A man came, unfortunate bridge. Tiresias:
with his dangerous memory come to the city of heroes.
Foolish man, looking for a woman

to watch her say again, go away.
Melting memories into dreams with a blind longing,
the hot longing that opens darkness,
melting the dreams of heroes into memories,
aching, aching.

*

A man arriving is an emissary or an enemy.
Tiresias holds his poor broken heart under the shedding jacaranda
as the heroes undo him in questions.

"Tell us the story of the war we won."
Like children looking for a history to wear.

What do I remember? Standing in the sun for hours listening
to speeches while my feet burned on the ground. Walking
along streets where women stood at every door crying.
Hacked bodies. A little man who followed me for three
kilometres and when I finally tried to grab him he begged me
to teach him to sing, but I thought he was lying and killed
him. A baby with its stomach carved out and a policeman
standing next to it, vomiting. Being given a computer and told
to write. The smell of beer on dead men's lips. Sitting in a
shebeen drinking brandy after brandy and getting so happy I
felt like flying. A woman laughing as another woman's house
burned down. Yellow cars and vans: that thick flat yellow
like sweet icing on a cake. The noise of helicopters. My
mother saying don't go, or don't come back. My child
screaming when I tried to pick him up. Meat roasting at my
child's funeral. A book with my photo in it. Crowds
becoming silent. A man who shot his wife in a meeting. The
noise of helicopters. My burning feet. Bodies in the street
covered in blankets.

My home is a place I'm frightened of. It's a big sore inside
me that burns when I touch it.

"Are you not bigger than your own backyard?
In that war each of us became the nation:
the whole nation entered into each of us.
Tell us that story."

That story. That story:
In Sharpville your arms died.
In Uitenhage your tongues died.
In Boipatong your eyes died.
In Katlehong and Bekkersdal and Empangeni you died and
you died and you died.
That's what I remember.

In Pretoria your fingernails became joint chief of staff.
In Pretoria your teeth ran the central bank.
In Pretoria your hair was the president.
That's what I remember.

In Jo'burg your heart was tortured and died.
In Cape Town your skin joined the enemy police.
In the veld and the mountains your memory buried its children.
That's what I remember.

That's what I remember.
All this dead and defeated, is your story.
Only the hair and the shadow still growing,
responding to sunlight, and I ask myself
which body were they grafted onto, in that moment of darkness
before total victory was declared?
My home is a place I'm frightened of.

The heroes leave him in the marketplace
like an old newspaper, blurred with the story of his heart,
sifting the dry breeze for her scent.

Robert Berold

DARK CITY

Dark city, houses standing noiselessly,
sun between the mountains, the whole earth
red with carnage. In the open space
inside your heart the bodies lying slaughtered.

Next morning you are calm again, well rested,
but there's last week's newspaper, those
nightmares are all true, people were shot down,
their bodies left to dribble in the dust.

Slow walks as sunset settles on these hills.
A praying mantis left her eggs on the moon.
You shout out to your god to take this darkness out of you –
these splintered darknesses embedded everywhere.

TWO MEDITATIONS ON CHUANG TSU

I

Evening. Thatch of sunset.
From the West End Record Bar:
mbaqanga. And the dry wind
burns with sound. Dlamini,
pretending madness, howls
in front of his brazier.
Washman stumbled from Malawi
into the neon fires of hell.
Soweto, Joburg's shadow, sleeps:
thin walls, you cannot trust
your neighbour. And do not
believe in history.

In ancient times, wrote Chuang Tsu,
men were happy without "doing good,"
they helped each other without "loving their neighbour"
they did not distinguish between great and small deeds
therefore they had no history.

The last train edges out.
The last wind weaves the lights.
Morning, lighting up the leaves,
will set alight the windows, shining
for an instant on the history within us,
the ancestors we've banished to our dreams.

II

January, a Monday, of the turning year.
Everyone's gone home already
in Tshayingwe's bus.
In the golden light, me and Wally
rake our weekend for insights.
Nothing but the same slow trudging
to imagined light.

Chuang Tsu, in Merton's version, wrote:
The purpose of the net is to catch fish,
when we have the fish we may forget the net.
The purpose of words is to catch ideas,
when we have the meaning we may forget the words.
I'd like to meet the man, he said,
who has forgotten words.

I quote this now to Wally as we lock up,
switch on the alarm. Driving home, the veld grass
has the sheen of autumn twilight.
I speak to Chuang across the centuries:
what would you have made of this place and this century
where everyone's so certain of their ideology?

He does not answer. In the greying light the veld
ablaze with feathery abundance,
of itself, for everyone.

PRAISE POEM

for pollen,
wet ferns,
sturdy insects,
for all tumbling
feelings,
for cool shale,
for layers of sea,
for fire,
for renewal,
for helium,
for blue plumbago,
rock cuttings
and railways
balancing on rivers,
for ball bearings,
for the seabird's clavicle,
for the benzene key
opening carbon's
lock to life,
for stone mulches,
for the mind of earth:
inscriptions of rosy succulents,
lettering of spiral flowers,
for the oxbow turn
on the Fish River,
for hungry bacteria,
for silver dunes,
for sudden mist,
for gooseflesh.

233

There is a mouth opened in me, a river
it flows down from my throat to the ground
through streams more liquid than water.

As I walk past the people passing in the rain,
this river, which is not mine,
flows into theirs.

It travels to some through the waves of air,
to some through the painful way they walk,
to some through the long bible of their thinking,

even the man who swings onto the bus
as it moves away. The township hisses,
it's a ribbon of smoke now.

There's a river in me, and it's not mine,
it was shown to me by a teacher of rivers,
and it flows and flows with its kirlian fire

then it falls and joins with others in their stream.
I am disappointed in people, but I love them more
and my hand is open at the place of the rivermouth.

MEET ME

meet me where the rhebok
whistle across the frost   meet me
where the moon crosses its fingers

touch me with your little infinity
lean me against   your laughter
push me off my ladder of expectation

meet me in the bush of wood-owls
wash me in your thirsty skin
clothe me in your shirt of anger

invite me to your house   invite me
strip me of my name   my gender
embrace my earth   my ash   my fire

THOSE DAYS

One died in a white bed   clutching metal
one saw only roses   another maps of stars
Death's suitcase was waiting   heavier each minute
packed in the hallway   ready to go

Where did it come from?   from too much money
too many bullets fired in laughter
It came with a flash of arterial blood
surprising the brain and drenching the lungs

It came with a chaos of swarming questions
invading the suburbs and trees of the city
It lived off bones and sourgrass and treebark
roasting domestic animals for food

It spread its mirrors   its floods of dry hunger
sieving the deserts   polishing the sands
It dropped diseases from distant aeroplanes
nothing flowed but the memory of rivers

Kelwyn Sole

POEM FROM BOTSWANA

The dogs here are a miserable crowd:
lean, incapable, bones pointing like fingers
through the yellow grass of their skin, turning over
hundreds of dustbins in search of a face.
They scream when kicked and cringe
and beg for food but do nothing ever useful.

No person in my village otherwise notices them,
which is what the dogs want most of all.

I have watched them die in ditches.
Three hundred yards from my house
one decays day after day, quietly.
His fur is a grey stain on the changing season:
the children grimace and hold their noses going past,
but that does not stop him being death.

They know, much better than we, how much
their flesh lives in a world of murder.
I listen at night to their anxious calling,
how they will not let the righteous sleep.
Their bodies turn in the volcano sky
bright as the stars to which they lift their heads.

I wait for the apotheosis of the dogs,
for the time they will exist, calloused and unrepentant,
when the holy and the damned have gone.

1

It is said that mankind
comes from Omumborombongo, that's
                    at Kaoho,
and there is a very large tree
and there is a hole

and it is the origin of men

and men when they come
                    to the O
they have fire and sacrifice there
and call upon it

                    and he
who passes in front
may not pass again in front
                    with a man
unless he die, may he not blaspheme
when he reaches the tree.

Here some sacrifice glass
and iron bead collars
but others, more generous, give
of their animals

and we, as we hear you,
hear you there by the sea
there in Kaoho
it is called omundjavaira
where our smoke of purgation
squeezes up

where the small cattle
came out of a rock,
and the oxen
and the living beings
that are among men

but these things are told
like a mystery:

2

out near
the desert of the Namib,
we are told
        by others
God has his home:
the sands shift and bite back
into the wind,
covering his Presence
        and then
coyly lifting the veil.

His beard is a kokerboom.
It is useless for anything
but tourists' cameras.

If you reach there
he will turn into a pool of water

if you kneel down
to drink the pool of water, it
will prove to be a mirage

if you look through your male fingers
at the mirage, you will see

your own face.

MANKUNKU

Dark golden boat
                on a sea
far away, rock with me
rock with me:

deep-throated bird
gentle me home
past the mud-lined street
where thoughts stick fast
and children pick rubbish
hungrily

the night flakes notes
from the scalp of my sorrow –

hide in my pillow
and cry for me

THE NATIONAL QUESTION

I want to grow quiet
as the earth.

I want to nod my head
in sleep, slowly,
cradled in its orbit
of dreams

where the stars
are a pattern
stitching the pillow:

I want my death
to be a mole that
burrows, ever burrows
under the property
of your beliefs

so that you
cannot find me, so that
you cannot purge me
from the soil
on which you stand.

WOMAN, TRESPASSING IN A GARDEN

During the week it's empty mostly
except for the hulking shadow
of the gardener, paid (poorly)
hourly, once every Tuesday,
steering his definitions
between hedge and flower-bed
with hosepipe and secateurs.

As soon as he's gone
                    without fail
a thin form
lurches up the road
stinking of oil and rubber
past the sonority of machismo brakes
in her knitted purple earcap
with a faded crimpoline dress
flapping much too large

picks her way carefully
through the tangled wire fence

as the wind plays with her hem
the way a dog would worry
                a tattered toy, to show
her red and bloated legs
to the no one who might be interested

her ritual is the same

collapsing on the grass
luxuriously drunk to sleep it off,
she dreams she is in a garden
with flowers ululating cerise and white
about her

then wakes
to find her fancy real.

Her thoughts remain composed. She
sits with face uplifted
to the warmth and the mountain
ridged and runnelled as a crust
of crumbling bread in front of her,
its involutions smeared with sun
a drooling ethereal honey

and for the hour she can safely rest

while her stale fingers fumble mealie
meal from the meths-stained
jam tin in her lap
                jagged there

lilies watsonias inebriate
the jaded taste of bees
birds quarrel with each other
and, fruit-demented, with the sky

spiders dance to trace their webs
and even the vaunting weeds dirge
to their shame of persecution

as once a week

through her aberrant presence
the garden is transformed
to more than a rich man's property.

HOMECOMING

You said come out of the shadows
come out of hiding
and we came
inch by inch
into the glare of borrowed klieg lights
into a country trying to sing in
harmony through its four separate channels
and you measured our attenuated muscles
our mouths sagging away from
the memory of a hunger
we could no longer name
you dressed us in swazi print in linen
shook our hands
we tried again and again
to tell our unheroic story
but your bouquets nodded fast
pinned to our dressing room mirrors
and we swam into a tropic
of banknotes and adulation
but soon
tripped by our own shadows
fell below your sight

into this darkness
multiplied across a nation
these small rooms

where you no longer
can find us to praise
and to betray

HOUSING TARGETS

Somewhere in our past
we believed in the future

that a better world
would discover foundation
under our feet, and we
would be forever singing,
in its kitchen.

Bricks pile up in a field.
Whether they will be enough
no one knows. How
they fit together
is anyone's guess.

Men with darkening skins
scribbled on by weather
wait for their instructions.

From time to time
limousines miraculously appear:
there is always a somebody
in a suit willing to smile
and shake their hands

who lays the first stone.

Then the camera lights
and racing engines
turn around, shrink back
from where they came.

Those left behind
stare at their own hands
afterwards, puzzled
at precisely what
has been transacted, why
they are still being offered
bonds

       squint
between gnarled fingers
pace out the hopeful distances:
 – there will be a flower bowl.
 – my bed is going here.

As for now the doorknobs
have no doors.

Their windows peer out
at no sky.

TAMED

You come out onto the dais,
distant as a god, a totem, raise
your arms and we roar
with an adoration like a rage.
But the trees are dumb,
the wind stalled, the air
ambivalent as a new wine.
There should be doves
to racket up in a salute,
but even the pigeons,
crouched on the windowledges, ring
us with their stricken rigid wings.
I strive
to tiptoe, to see
you the better, but my blood,
like the wind, has stalled
and I am mired in the flesh
turned slush of my feet as my fists
pump the air and I shout
old slogans old gods
hear as but the cold
seas' mechanical praise.
Beside me, a black
man in glasses, moustache's
white-as-a-milk-
slick waiting to be tongued,
face falling in,
turns to me his back
in its suit of a fine cloth,
frets behind the glasses, hooks
out a single shining tear.
Hemming me, two
louts with wet lips, eyes hot
as coals a wind blows

to this side of flame,
still their roistering, stand
imploded and intent,
agelessly beyond their age.
One looks up, around
him, seeing only you,
and his face lights
with something of the sublimity
he must believe you bring,
beneficently will lend.
Your hand cuts,
and it silences us
as though it severed tongues,
and I am looking back to the once
the hand held mine
and it was still the man's
the sourness of the cells
gloved with the sourness of a death,
and your eyes were still those
of one running from the long hell.
And now?
Are you still he that,
stripped to his soul,
denied it its death,
sought the dream in even stone and iron?
A mannikin hands
you the typed sheets of your speech.
You shuffle them, tap
the microphone, gently clear
an old phlegm from your throat –
and are oracle,
measured thunder of your voice
doomsday's in a square.
But then comes
the small fumble of the tongue,
the stretching thin

of the fabric of the spell,
and the words are sad
old slogans that fall
like stones onto a stone,
and I see now the white,
imperial quiff is blued,
though the eyes
still scuttle in an old skull,
and the mannikin is feeding
you with more words,
stolidly as into a machine,
and a dignitary lifts
a cuff to check a watch,
to covertly signal now
is the time to ring
down the curtain, move
on to a new square in an old game.
You heed.
We rise in rapture, stretch
up our hands to the kitsch,
alienating pedestal we've piled
for your pinioning, and you reach
out to bless
us and I am hanging my head –
amongst these many thousand others
hanging my head lest
you see me weep,
knowing, as I know,
that there is no crying like
the lamentation of old men.

I went to Anton Fransch's funeral:
he held off the police for seven hours.

The minister
with careful logic sketched
a parable of ancient Babylon:
I savoured the aptness of the simile
but thought of Africa,
the photograph I had seen the night before:
a buffalo being dragged down by hyenas,
one eye ripped out, the bloodied muzzle
agape and bellowing.

Lately flushed
out of the closets of his ambivalence,
well-fleshed beneath the robes
of his unaccustomed Arabism,
the minor community leader droned
predictable pomposities,
eyes darting that way, this,
reminding me of the cockroach that,
when we had ripped up the floorboards of my tottering hovel,
had rushed about with kamikaze unstoppability,
seeking the sullen lair we,
and the sunlight,
had violated.

Only the advocate,
with customary shrewdness, traversed
a more accommodating territory,
not striving for the pinnacles of the professionals,
targeting not the dead son but the still living, disposable mother,
persuading from me one reluctant teardrop.

On the march,
we held the flag up with both our hands,
they having taken our staff for the great flag
roaring like a godswind about the fragments
of Anton Fransch in the box that held nothing but them,
only the voice living on, perhaps,
in a heart or the earth's groaning.

Four round housewives of Bonteheuwel
fled from the hot sun
in the flag's fluttering shadow,
using it as a sunshade,
shimmying and chattering only of that
which housewives customarily chat about,
gossiping over companionable fences.

We boarded the bus:
we were alone amongst children.
On the staircase behind me,
a boy and a girl touched,
slyly rather than shyly,
eyes rapacious rather than radiant
with the incontinent passion of their puberty.
The bus belched:
then moved and shuddered
to the pounding of fists, thudding of boots
of children grown suddenly, frighteningly ageless,
screaming obscenities at gathering squad-cars,
blue-bodied, imperviously watching
riot-squad policemen,
flags snapping and snarling, wind howling.
In the coffin,
the new, the sacred reliquary,
the handful of flesh and bone and sinew
that for seven improbable hours challenged
all the paraphernalia of power, shaming

them and us,
equally.

I went to Anton Fransch's funeral:
Did the tongues fall short because the tongue
cannot take the citadel?
Did the buses shudder
only with our hatred,
or the anguish also at our own inadequacy?
Did the four round housewives of Bonteheuwel
chatter only in their mindlessness,
or as birds do
when the serpent moves in the wasteland?

Anton Fransch was a very heavy hero:
I think, sometimes, we dropped him along the road somewhere,
and he lies there still,
in the seeding grasses,
the bright, blue moonlight,
and only the beetles, swarming,
bury him.

THE TRAP

They phoned me at two in the morning.
I know because the moon,
quivering on the near horizon,
lit up the startled clock-face.
The voice was cold, authoritative.
"This is the police," it said.
"A man has been reported tampering with your vehicles:
please check on it."
Against my ear, the still open wires
whispered of cosmic spaces, faceless people.

I put the phone down, lay a moment,
swinging between night and morning,
the water in my drinking-glass
heavy as an oil of silver,
the clock's quiet ticking pacing
the moonlight on the hillside's glowing shoulder.
A lone car passed, heading into morning.
Silence washed back in the wake of it,
leaving me alone in a beleaguered city.
I thought of the voice on the telephone:
flat, toneless, authoritative.
Old habits die hard in old prisoners:
I rose, went to the kitchen, cracked aside the curtains.
The cars bulked below me,
grounded, ruminative, humped like sleeping cattle,
the mist rising from them
like the breath from bovine headlamps.
Nothing moved there:
only a cat that sped from under a warming chassis,
a cloud that dappled it with undulant shadow.
I stood, uncertain.
The skies leaned over me in burdened glory:
a breath would surely topple them,
strew the earth with flaming galaxies.
I went back to bed, stared
at the flaming silver water in my drinking-glass,
the throbbing, burning moonlight.
The phone rang again,
imperiously in imperial silence.
The voice was chill, cutting, edged with anger.
"Did you check the vehicles?" it asked.
"There is nobody there," I whispered.
Against my ear, the still open wires
hummed of cosmic spaces, faceless people.
I put the phone down, shaken by a sudden, soundless crying

as around the bend, beside the kitchen,
a soft starter-button swung an engine
and a car slid past with tinted windows.

THE MUGGING

The voice is right alongside:
so close, I cringe.
Can he have a match, it pleads.
He is young,
lean,
bowed a little
with the obsequiousness of one who needs.
Dark, with the black,
straight hair of a half-
caste Indian teen, he stares
slightly to one side,
correctly not meeting my eyes.
I give him the box,
tell him he can keep it,
relieved
at the meagreness of his demand.
He thanks me, falls behind:
I walk on.

It is late and I am going home
across the wasteland where once I lived.
White with stars,
the sky
wraps me round;
its light gilds
the myriad faces of small stones
that roll under my shoes,
silvers dry,

winter grasses rustling high
as my thighs.
He is on my back,
bearing me to the ground;
the breath bursts from me like air
from a ruptured balloon:
I feel the skin
peel away from my knees.
Others are rising now,
like leopards, from the stones,
pinioning me with hot,
predatory hands.
His knife glitters, bright
as the beyond-the-city,
beautiful stars,
ludicrous as my unseemly sprawling here.
The blade nicks my throat,
steadies in a small,
silent pool of pain.
The others strip me
of clothing, shoes;
their hands move about me
like devil-lovers' hands,
shocking into sensitivity
my serene, celibate skin,
flopping aside even my genitals
with passionless aplomb.
Incredulously I hear
the knifeman plead:
sorry, biya, sorry,
but it's Christmas
and we must buy wine.
They find what they want
in my left sock's heel:
little plastic bag
bound with a rubber band –

last of my week's wage.
The knife lifts, then, and they rise
from the offal of my bones,
fade into the night,
easily as clouds,
trailing a faint scent
of sweat and young skin.

Am I still here,
stones troubling my spine,
grass-stem sticking in my eyes,
or does this naked, lonely body run
with them over the harsh,
desperate lava of the land?

WHO WERE YOU?

Muddied, slow brown sea
rolling onto, sliding over
wafers of white sand:
I think of you, your turning
the brown belly of your love to me,
its languid sweetness welling in
the tidal-sleek
dark cupping of your thighs,
your breasts,
lustrous as two aubergines,
sinuously sliding under
my pale skin.

High up in the cloud-
bespattered sky, seething
wind-disordered trees,
a bird is ringing

thin and silver bells of song:
I hear again
the circling, searching wind that wound
about us strands
of pale and clinging air,
the thunder of my heart, the blood
cascading in my ears,
a cricket shrilling somewhere under leaves.

Who were you that turned
your body all to mine,
no unguents on it, nor perfumes,
no trailing weeds of tresses for my hands,
ashes, rather, as of grass, its
blackened stubble for your hair,
twin agates your two eyes,
as old the stone
of flesh below
the lissom skin, your gaping mouth
the screaming plover's when
the last thrust comes?

CAT ON A HIGH YARD WALL

You wake up in the dark, day far,
and the trees trembling in the chill sea-breeze,
but silently, old leaves showering,
and the cat walking on the high yard-wall,
assured, small paws carefully placed
in impossible glass and rough, crushed stone,
shoulders sloped in the easy ambling
of the lion that's never far below,
and then the gathering, the incredible leap,
straight up, onto a higher level of the wall,

257

and the insouciant sauntering on,
unmindful of your humiliation at such
a contemptuous showing-off of grace.

You stretch your legs, thinking of the cat,
that endless, effortless, stretching leap,
but dry joints crack and you are suddenly
flat on your feet on the cold cement,
dancing like a manic marionette,
old man's muscles stretched too tight.
Tiredly, you lean against the high yard-wall,
wet with the pain of your knotted calves,
and the far-off moon looks down on you,
and hurts, as the cat so hurt, because
its beauty is unapproachable and it does not care.

It is then that you face what no man does
unless it is the middle of the night and the day far:
you are old and dry as these dry leaves
and the road that once seemed endless is
turning through its last slow curve,
and you can cry if you want to, and be a fool,
because the road, like the cat, has never cared.

As none have ever really cared,
neither lovers nor friends: all loose your hand
at the final bend of the road.
You call to them, but they turn away
in terror of your end.
The cat, though, still walks along
the high yard-wall, and you watch it go.
Where, in your heart, the grace to leap,
like it, straight up, to a higher plane?

I am looking back a long way now:
will the circle close?
Why does the city this morning seem
so much like that other city,
its lines imposed upon its lines:
the same slow sweep of waves,
the same dust-haze,
the same crumbling buildings sinking into the salt sea,
the same sad, unstoppable malaise:
this garden I pause beside,
its dahlias sun-dried,
the nasturtiums neutered,
a solitary palm-tree bending towards Siwa,
begging its moisture
as little and as bitter as urine on the sand –

nothing dies:
all that I thought long-dead
is rising up again:
the little house where first they slapped me into life,
took off the tip of my manhood as the religion demands,
the red sand slipping into the blue Mediterranean,
the smell of incense on the khamsin wind –
so much remembered,
so many old lamps burning again –
lamps whose wicks I thought had long since charred –
and from the night beyond their light
a face is floating,
bending over mine –
its sweetness is effulgence,
its fragrance is of flowers . . .

SOLITARY CHILD

With acknowledgements to St. John of the Cross

"Hold the plank," he'd say,
building the house.
"Don't jiggle it."
But he would jiggle it,
sawing with the short,
harsh thrusts of one
who copulated or raged,
lopping me off from him with the iron
teeth of his iron,
applying no balm
of that which was alien to iron,
leaving it to time to staunch
the bleeding though
still I bleed,
old fool, now, with an old pain.
It took half a day
to walk around the farm,
walking fast, dog at my heels,
furthest boundary the last
of the rivers of legends and lies.
Nobody walked
with me there: neither he
nor she of the shadows and shy eyes.
There were others once:
aliens my age with alien ways.
We tore
into each other like hounds, were dragged,
howling, apart, and I was back
in the aloneness I never knew
had a name that was not mine.
He beat me for that:
did not stop when I said

it had been because of the tree.
My tree.
What else to love,
he being no loving man?
"They carved their names in my tree,"
I said, and spoke
as of a fouling of a shrine.
But I did not cry and he beat
me the harder, but the strap
snapped on the brute
bark of my back, and she looked
through the window and wept
the tears I could not find.
Small, grey child fled then,
climbed up, very high,
into the old tree, laid
a cheek to the rough,
sweet bark as to a skin.
Did that many times and,
now and then,
like this old man with his old pain,
very softly sang.

NIGHTRIDER

At the mountain's top, I reach up,
I fill my haversack with stars. .
I am at the centre of the soundless night,
my bicycle's light alone still warms.
How wan that warmth,
how vast the cold that moves
through last year's long dead grass.
Always my dynamo's humming on the wheel
seems such a very winter sound.

Through many a long night it has followed me
up many a long hill, the white moonlight
spilling over us, white as the sea's foam.
Ah, that sea! roaring hugely
out of the huge night,
rearing on the black rocks below.
How tiny my cycle's light,
how minuscule my soul.

SUNDAY NIGHT – ON MY OWN – AFTER THE UITENHAGE SHOOTINGS

There is not much doubt, tonight,
                              if I could paint I would not
be writing, but painting the
                              night air, the sweet wind, tonight.

At first I longed to paint trees,
                              like gums, or maritime pines,
on open squares like on the
                              flats – Italian ochre and
palpable thick-veined olive;
                              but it is the air, through the
green, across the flats, blowing
                              the balm of thick night air that
makes me want the soft stroke on
                              canvas, thick layers of air,
smelling of lemon, blown through
                              pine needles, blown through
   pepper
trees in the square here in this
                              Observatory, blowing
the mobile gentle birds at
                              my barred window, ignoring
me, not minding, I can go
                              on writing wanting to paint
the wind so soft, tender as
                              a contented mother or
confident lover, him-self,
                              wholly, tolerating this
my wanting to blow away,
                              to still, the week's anxious fear;
it stirs despite the people
                              killed this week, despite carnage,

breathes despite the dead, despite

                              murder, inability
of the weak to keep death fixed

                              in front of body, being
mind, despite desire for god

                              of gentle wind, balm of night;

by the day's light tomorrow
they will have stopped the mourning;

and the wind will rip again
exposing

                no time

                      for balm.

TREES SKY SPACE

hope not being hope
until all ground for hope has
vanished
– Marianne Moore

            until you find yourself functioning
            in a rhythm of forgetfulness,
            not bothering to glance up at the
            clouds streaking crepuscular cerise
            across blue, through the bathroom window,
            above sweaty hay-heads of your kids;

            until you find yourself head down to
            routine repetition, no glimpse of
            recreation, world recreating
            itself in quotidian splendour,
            neighbour's wild strelizia dancing
            with masked weavers, flying to plunder

meticulously, strip by strip, your
bamboo, outside the bathroom window,
head to tail, squadrons darting, black, gold,
getting houses in order for chicks,
so intent they do not notice you
notice them through the bathroom window;

until you forget to keep looking,
keep taking joy, until you feel your
muscles seize down your back with bending,
you forget why poems bother to
celebrate restoring movement, trees
sky space.

DOVE

Peripheral, exhausted, washed out
onto the shore of dreams
like a ribbon of sea-weed
the figure lies splayed.

This is no gold coast
no beach of bronze langour
of sun-seeped sand.
This is the tawdry sub-tropical
strip at the edge of the tepid sea.

I think I shall turn to religion:
not Christ – I am tired
of failed saviours –
only the cool incense breath of the holy spirit,
the dark anonymity of the nave,
yes, the comforting womb of the church;
I think I shall

fall there prostrate, wings splayed,
hard red breasts pressed against the pew,
on a Monday morning
(when the baby's asleep,
his sister at playschool),
the woman sweeping the church
thinking I am struck down with devotion,
or, seeing, sideways,
the flight of worn-out spirit of woman;
then maybe the church words will soothe
my barbed feathers;
cool pebbles washed by the sea;
no; I doubt it;
I think I shall have to make my own prayer
for the quotidian demands of hard day – swill it round
like pills with black coffee –
no; make it, rather,
mouths full of muffins at my mother's breakfast
breaking the night;
night of spectres of dead aspirations and
the baby crying and
crying, coo to me caressing voice
give me warm milk and
deep sleep again
deep sleep;
there in the cool of the church
I shall chew my rough words,
my coarse-grained words,
spirits of women give me patience
and love to unblock the ducts
of love for my children, conduits
of love for the father
of my children;
inject me with potency
to wipe away this anaesthetic veil
keeps me from entering life lightly again;

give me strength to remember my love,
give me love –
no; I shall not pray for transfiguration,
for centuries long, long ago longing for peace
of Madonna and Child;
less, less, give me less, only
strength for the tasks
of love.

GHAZAL

We are beyond Molly Bloom.
We are beyond redemption.

Sperm that is soft and salty in the mouth
becomes sharp and bitter as it bites the throat.

Men may be different in some ways,
but all sperm tastes the same.

Orion's belt, a star-studded whip,
flogs the bony sky.

My eyes are simply skewered slits
blinded by lust and celestial brightness.

The eye of the penis is always round and howling
ever eager for release from its hydrocephalic head.

The red cherries on your plate
are both intensely sour and deeply sweet.

No one at the cafe knows why we speak so much and eat so little,
nor why every satisfying sex act is recalled as a small miracle.

The sea is so dark at night and the rocks seem so sharp,
but we rush to the water with brave hearts and bare feet.

The stars are breathless and do not sing.
My mouth waters even in my dreams.

As I came in the moonlight
I saw your ribs
suddenly stand out of your skin
and glow in the dark
like the long strands
of a string instrument.

So I ran my fingers down your chest
and plucked the strings,
my curling lips clicking and singing
sucking the sap of your bone,
slowly honing into the song of your soul,
that bursts its whiteness into my womb.

Cathy Zerbst

Dusk
   calls the shadows in
     like whales

Magnolia blue
   eerie in the flattened pitch
     of twilight

You pull me in
   crush my mouth like leaves
     make the whole earth buckle, tilt and spring

The spinning sky opens
   its trapdoor
     lets the violet in

I cling to you
   like fading light
     in April

Love you
   lose you
     overnight

Johann de Lange

KOOS PRINSLOO [1957-1994]

I

Death is the passing .. of a living being into what Christian Boltanski
calls "an absolutely disgusting pile of shit."
– Didier Semin

Death, Didier Semin wrote in *An artist of uncertainty*,
is the passing of a subject into the state
of an object; the passing of a human being
into a thing; of a friend
into a corpse, a stranger:
3 o'clock in the morning,
the hour of garbage cans
and jingling milk bottles,
they took away your gaunt blind body
in a black body bag.
The slaughtered morning,
still bloody and shivering.
The hour of carcasses
grimacing on meat-hooks,
of buttocks quivering on the butcher's block,
when the saws sing piercingly
at the abattoirs, and stray dogs
yelp around the entrails.

The morning after your death
the papers reported black
on white only the bare facts.
Three columns and a photo.
But it's another image
that haunts me: the rectum as a grave.

II

In the Great Rift Valley, the genesis,
and the Kudiakam pan

where baobab trees once burned
as in a dream and the lioness
crouches drinking attentively;
underneath the pink tufts
of the wild chestnut bushy
with drooping old man's beard,
domain of the timid-grey dik-dik,
of "thousands upon thousands of wildebeest
braying and bellowing, their hooves
thundering across the dusty plains,"
in the pitchgreen valleys and forests,
invisible and frail, your nemesis hides.

III

My eyes roam you Africa
your Masai Mara like a green skin
with clearings like pores
torn green shirt of Africa
my volcanic Africa
rough elephant hide of lava Africa
black sarcoma Africa
Rift Valley and ashen escarpment Africa
my tectonic restless Africa
Africa with the string of lakes
round her wrinkled throat
Africa of the fickle rivers
with rain brief as infatuations
dwindling into riverbeds
Africa your indecipherable soul
Africa of steppes savannahs and forests
Africa of flame-tree and bluegum
Africa bleeding through a river-mouth
mute Africa

receive your fair-haired son
joined to a plasma-bag and memories
the frightened child in gaunt pajamas and confusion

translated from the Afrikaans by the poet

Ari Sitas

EVENING TIDES I

When the sun sets behind KwaMashu and further back past the
thousands of hills and the cattle are herded
and the children are rustled inside
and the mothers count them again removing thorns, lice, birdshot
with caring hand

and we feel alongside our shoulders making sure that our head
still weights our neck down right through our spine
and the descending grey disappears the sharkfin, the boatyard, the
casspir
we are left with only our fiercer loves
and the sounds of hooks that we tear out from each other's
hearts.

ETHEKWINI

There is
        an expanse of green and dust
        hemmed-in
                by cane and a stitchwork of hills
there, here,
        this expanse
                spat at by waves
                pummeled by sunblasts
                        stewing in sweat
                        yes, liquid
                        yes, waves: whose necks are
                                        thickset with corrugation
there, here
        is this expanse that claims me: my Hell.

From here
        from this hell's odours
                – tomato street, guava avenue, molasses valley
                steel-shavings township, glue location, massala hill
                        melting and boiling –
        there is no stench of heaven left to prize
                there is a sky: yes –
                        blue-like, grey-like, alien-like
                                weighing downwards
                                pouring
                                sweat
                                        at dusk
                                                downwards
                                riveting all aground
                        downwards, yes,
                with only sideward escapades.
There, here,
                mechanical bullfrogs and cicadas grind away
                and sometimes wounded cars cough-by pierced by
        assegais
                and sometimes surfers emerge from the mouths
        of microwave ovens

                and always
                        life continues like the sound of splintering glass

This hell,
        hemmed in:
                its forced geometry of concrete boils
                spread outwards
                        sidewards
                                in its rashes of sack cloth
                                of shack, of specification matchbox
                                to touch the stitch work of hills
                        as near the docks
                                the boss drives by in his Shepstone Benz
                                as his "boys" load Cetshwayo's skull as cargo

here, there,

    confined

        where visions of heaven subsided long ago
        with the arrival of sails creaking
           under a hyperload of sparrows

here,

    there,

      in this maze of splintering glass
        in this expanse that claims me
          in these infernal flamewaves tanning my fate
         I was lost there
        smiling
          porcelain smiles
      and waving
         ox-hide kites.

SIX SECTIONS FROM SLAVE TRADES

I had them strap a seat and lift me up
my body swelling, rotting in the sun
and march me down the twisted, acrid paths
to take me down to sea.

They shall count us after the flood and we shall still be two
I thought
After the flood we shall be counted two by two
I thought
but deep inside I knew that Africa had all its wiser ways
and on the road, the bone and the shrub cut deep inside my soul
They shall count us one by one astride our lonely beds
or else they shall not find us when the counting starts
and we shall dwindle off with just our putrid breathing

and cut the landscape up
    not with our plough, or flower or heart
        but with an axe.

                *

I saw him lifted up, his face – flabby, loose, distended
his songs long forgotten,
lost in the fevers of his infernal sorrows
and his shroud, lean, threadbare and his colonies of slaves
sinking in the mud
his dreams floating down, down towards the Red Sea
his soft parts pulped, reeking the foulest of desires
and his hide – only a fish's sheen
his sheen a fish's scent.
His hirelings buckled under his weight
edging forward
a funerary bulk
moving past the ostrich's, the camel's, darting, bluegrey eyes.

                *

I remember most of all his hands, large, larger than language,
stubborn hands, sturdier than a Harari horse
and his spoor of stale garlic, of ever-reeking sweat
plastered up in perfume
and his flannel underwear, I do remember grimy and his eyes
darting out haunted by the steps of perky Arab boys

I remember his hands and the gift of whiteman's disease and
semen
in my loins
and he laughed at me – "you truly believe in God?" he used to
tease as he held on to twist my nipple
holding the writ that made me his

for eighty guns,

        between his legs

                *

I woke up to face another day in this house
I saw the ravages of our estate once too often
   the chipped mortar, brick and of course as always, the ash
I walked over the trinkets and the cracked remnants
and urged to go to find one who could finally destroy
who could finally rebuild our house
for I was weak, weakened by the day
and they were many
I sold her off for eighty guns
and all the guns for sailor's cloth
And I walked off with my sail wrapped around my head
against the cruel sun.

There must be a trail, I said, leading out of this land of infamy
and barter – a road
friendly to shoe-leather or sail;
   to leave, yes – not through the fancies and the landscapes of
      the mind
   to leave, yes – the fences of this reasonable world
   and its iced thinkings
   and the chattering of all its nimble poets
   to bid a final farewell to this horrid rack
where my words dried out
from the harshness of your trading winds.

I am to leave this house,
this garden
I am to leave these words behind
and all their well-wrought meanings

I am to struggle to be mute again
I am to leave these lurid coastlines
– Europe, Aden, Natal, Ithaca or more

*

The roadside curb was to be my bed, and my rucksack
slanting off a startip's point above, and the spinning sky my
shelter and I remember how my head wined and romantic felt
her face, become the moon during those indigo-tinted nights

The birds of prey would tune my song the dovecote's crap my
aroma my tattered boot and lace would be my harp, to
serenade her yellow glow to comfort me against the dreads
and spooks of nighttime

Come closer you wenches I'd cry drunk come closer I'd sing,
male or female, come trample on all of my casks of woe it's
for you I make rhymes torn or frail it's for you, you pieces of
mutton or tripe that I strum at my leather and pretend to grow
a feeling more felt than a gruesome pustule

Often at night on the grass by the roadside, I'd rest my head
on your hairy belly, on your smoothsoft skin, on your heaving
flab and listen to the hairs growing out of your moist skin to
pierce my earlobe and my hand on your thigh and the
moonlight dribbling light on the furrows of your back, your
front, catching us guilty us, of unclean compassions

But then again the bird would tune my song, our minds would
criss-cross desert sands, I'd sing of how I carried you along
upon my shoulders kissing your scented hands and saving the
taste of your skin inside my heart

The roadside curb was to be my bed and the choirs of heaven
my echoes, – the angels, fat, obese, howling heavenly hymns

279

in my stupor, their jaws striking out as gross as the yelps of
my beaten but comradely dogs, as gross as my life was then,
as gross as it is now and out of kelter

Come closer you wenches, my dreams, come closer.

*

Come here, follow me past the markets of Addi-Abbi
past my ancestral homes
where the older gods stirred thunderclouds with vengeance
and where the new one hammered on wood is
guarded by shrill, austere monks and parchment
come, here, look at the footprints
and the marks all creatures formed as traces in the mud
here: the guinea fowl and deer
here: come, the zebra stumped a hoof and here: a lioness and
    cubs have littered here
come, follow me down to the canyon's forked fingers
that point you down and shove you down to my valleys
look: left, the Semien range – pink, pink from all the snow
and harsh sunrays of my ancestral gods and later,
as the sun sets you will see how it makes the clouds
around its nose look like dark clerical hats on fire
now red, now redder, now redfire-coloured
Slide down the little waterfall with me
the rainbow
in the trickle will not hurt you
here,
        run through the coffee garden
past the fruittrees and the flowers
smell how my people cook the thick banana on open fires
look at these pomegranates, oranges, limes
and figs drying in the sun
come, let us run around the hill there
past the songs, boys and girls intone

twist with me past the bank of the Taccuzze river
come, here, by the tall poplars
here,
     you see, some of the footprints stop
here is
      the clubbing ground
the dented skulls heaped up just there
are of the ones who
were too lame to make it to the sea
to fetch a price, come, follow me,
see how the weather made them,
        how it makes them shine!

Sandile Dikeni

TRACK OF THE TRACKS

*for my brother, Dicey who died
of TB at the railways*

it begins
with a laugh
hard,
breathless as steel

Xhegwazana phek'ipapa
Xhegwazana phek'ipapa
Sayithath'apha
Sayibek'apha
Sayithath'apha
Sayibek'apha

Mama makes porridge
my granny makes porridge
take it here
put it there
take it here
put it there

there
the night comes sweating
perspiring outwards
drags the guts
in a blood red pulp
that drains the sweet
of youth

out
out to the harshness
of world
that leaves you cold

when sun
unveils generous blanket of light
but never touches
the inside of bone
and marrow shrivels
ice stone
inside
outside
inside the railway tracks
where we chant:

Sojikel'emaweni
emaweni
sojikel'emaweni
emaweni
sojikela'aphi na he?
he wee!
sojikela'aphi na he?
he wee!

We bend the cliffs
the cliffs
we bend the cliffs
the cliffs
we bend them for you
and you
hey you!

our breath is hot
like the hiss of Makadas
the steam train that puffs
against the winter wall
of a karoo drought
that bends, swerves

through our lives
black as the soot

from the coal mines of Newcastle
where some more black blood coughs
from deep down:
sishov'ingolovane
ngolovane
sishov'ingolovane
ngolovane

we push the small coal trains
against the winter's white breath
that cracks
under our boots
melts into ice crystals
hardens in our lungs' lobes
be we shall sing
warm longings:
Sdudla sibomvu
mathangan'abomvu
Sdudla sibomvu
mathangan'abomvu

my baby's hot
her thighs are red
my baby's hot
her thighs are red

sing, sing
until death comes,
sings,
in our breath.

Rustum Kozain

FAMILY PORTRAIT

Aunt May sways, rocks herself like a baby,
chafing her heart over worn linoleum, amongst
unhinged doors resting on the floor, shrinking
in the corner of my Ma's small kitchen.

She lives there now. Her husband imported
the latest lover, keeps her, with arrears
for buildings and new cars piling up.

Brother and cousin've bought guns
making babies with one eye open on
the back door. Old enough to afford it,
they are finally prepared, and wait
for a 20-year-old black onslaught.

Buckie and Mo are doped on mandrax.
Buckie robbed a bottle store, implicated
in his friend's suicide note. He still
drives the neighbourhood, waving at passers-by

Gail and her husband, two children strong,
still want to finish their studies; they
mention this everytime I wipe braaivleis juice
from the corners of my sardonic mouth.

Sonny's a principal carrying flattened joints
in his file, spinning out to a house empty
but for fishtanks, dogturds, a double mattress
and a friend's wife now his lover.

I've switched off, into loneliness
and light candles to this amber mood
driving drugs and loud music into me
dancing with my shadow bent into
the corners and ceilings of this room.

Ma says she's switched off too, can't
take the strain of everyone's problem
as the family close their eyes and stroke
their lashes according to the latest fashion.

The blood thicker than water runs thin
now holding our broken togetherness
all of us flung away from poverty.

FROM BROTHER, WHO WILL BURY ME?

Yes. I'll die. And grow quiet as the earth.
Buried in the pauper's graveyard in Paarl
Where the unknown and the wretched lie
In a rusty field, next to the meadow
Where horses stare at their future as petfood,
Close to where, after a fight with my brother,
To heal the hurt that he was bigger, stronger;
That I could never hope to win, with strength or reason,
I walked to heal that heartbreak.

Ten, I walked into the veld, sat next to a stream
Where the sound was all; not the whiffs
Of laundry and decay from upstream
Where the poor wash clothes and everything else.
In a bleached Coke can, I stuck a malaise of veldflowers,
Took them home to my mother and cried,
Sobbed in my frustration, unable to show her
The solace in the knowledge that one's alone,
Even as that solace hurts more.

Decades ago this field was a jumble of shacks.
Migrant workers, and their wives and children,
All without Passes, lived here, called it

Bongweni, favourite place. Shacks long razed,
People evicted, some caught crouching in rocks,
Like fossil waiting to spring into beginning
Here in this favourite place with its rows of graves

I want to lie here and feel other children
Tug at hardy veldflowers, rip solace from sods
And, even if their palms should bleed,
Offer my death to tearful, comforting mothers.

Mxolisi M. Nyezwa

BARRACKS

my ma says
too much of anything brings a man emptiness
too much thought
clogs the mind
too much fury
fails the heart

so too much of anything is an inner emptiness
too much love
pains the heart
too much sadness
wearies the bones

and inside the vacuums of our lives
the universe is a turntable
spinning endlessly

THINGS CHANGE

at least then, it won't be like this
it will be a totally new suffering
like when a baby sucks
his thumb

it will be a totally new experience
(for God and history has provided)
we won't have to blow our minds
about it

it will be like a fresh song
from a sparkling songbird
it will be like that for us, as an old
woman sits neglected

on the chair of her memories
it will be fresher, more vital
for us . . . at least it won't be like
death

and like the death that we die
every moment of our lives
it will be a totally new suffering
it will be like a song sung free
from a careless heart

(our failure will have its dignity).

I CANNOT THINK OF ALL THE PAINS

I cannot think of all the pains in men's breasts
without the urge to sleep, or to lie down, i cannot think
without seeing God's face in the child's smile,
or in the lonely cry in the night and in the sea.

I cannot think of all the pains that have come
and gone, pains in men's waists
and in men's shoes –
i cannot have relief proper, wearing a neat tie.

I run around in circles, like water sprinkling from a pipe,
i can't have true relief, swearing out loud,
and counting out the pains in my breast,
and in my pants.

I cannot think of all the pains and all the years wasted,
all the craze of lonely men in village rooms,
and all the bodies that lie out cold, in avoided streets –
i can't run out old, like a joyful child

and watch a sky pregnant with pain, or with turbulent rain,
i cannot think of the soil without lying down,
i cannot think of tears, lonely geographies
and the third world, without the urge to cry, or to sit down

Lesego Rampolokeng *aka Leroi Jones*

AFTER BRA W'S FLOWERS

(at the moment of rude awakening & rule taking)

let all mothers
behold the flowers
they defeat human hurricane
& unnatural powers
these flowers bloom
in the gloom of death's factory
now corpses stride
veins pulsating with martyr pride
now chartered freedoms come
to lives turned slum
lifting us above the mouse
gnawing the pillars of our father's house
now we climb from the basement
of son-god's abasement
now our history
moves out of its murder mystery
& RECITES
the poetry of strange sights
the images of mid-day nights
now we retrace
footprints disappeared without trace
on the backs of bullets
inside prison gullets
frozen in hot shells
fried in cold cells
& we ask
what form now does the storm take
after drinking from the blood lake?

IN TRANSITION

we spin in circles of terror
caught in cycles of a nightmare
of judgement
where the mirror
of the present
shows the face of error
in transition

when the rains come the fires die
yet we are warm
like lice on the pubis
in love time
singing cold bones
in the rain of hope
around the flame of red dawn
in transition

we whirl on our stand
kicking skulls on the soccer-field
& from the grandstand
applause rings in blood-drops
celebrating the abortion
of freedom's child
in transition

wailing around the burning tyre
we raise a sacrificial pyre
songs of struggle turn quacks
in the quagmire
in transition we wear our hearts
on the outside
in t-shirt fashion trend style
colourful speeches popular talk
of hypocrisy

292

by the graveside
in transition

it's an arty-farty-party
riding the back of genocide
somewhere a head cracks full of lead
& someone cracks a wise aside
it's all a fart in the wind
we leave behind
& run to hide with pride
at every stride
in transition

eating the brains of the dead unborn
how can we mourn the dead
wearing their umbilical cords around the neck
drunk on amniotic fluids
smiles glittering in the light
of chandeliers
of mind control
in transition

we are mutant legions
defining ourselves in noble terms
flaming placards at cold barricades
drawing safe lines behind crumbling walls
of euphoria ...
behind the blades of our own danger
in transition

petty bush pigs
talking about negotiation-table manners
fuckademics unrolling scrotals of fartastic words
to ennighten the illiterate
witches in churches
passing the collection goal

293

fools in schools
without mules
with whips for stools
& then tools
in transition

thus we rush to the future
unless the wheel of time
gets a puncture

FOR THE ORAL

intuitive it is instructive expressive
it is excessive flaming it is flailing hand
knowledge of the age it is rage too hot
for the page it is searing on the wing
it is pain on the stage spit sweat fart
cunt cock your gun invective it is what i said
& what you haven't heard censored in the night
& day inventive mass bounding it is binding
the heart in pieces it is blinding black
lightning bleeding through the mouth when
i shout vomiting bits of soul defecating
the faeces of my spirit ORAL it is moral
gut reaction purgation it is cleansing for
a social living purity it is superlative
super-charged kinetic it is MOTION in the word
unchained it is bounding across walls through
jail-bars it is burning in my bloodstreams
groundbased exploding leaves igniting roots
it is pulling at my dreadlocks it is bark on
FIRE action multiple barrelled at multitude
cannons it is man woman child non-animal killing
though they be human it is glaring at you between

the lines sharpening its teeth to chew your mind
it is mad psychopathic guilty before it's charged
& high charged bombs guns knives shooting through
right between my lips blowing my brains
it is beating eardrums
it is savage barbaric just jumped down a tree with dr alban
from a hot mouth
ORAL not a blow job though it goes for the top
or maybe it is if you're an academic
it's got yeats on heat fat sweat keats bubbling to the beat
rock the rhythm of this poem of the year shakespeare
your bigotry begets my poetry
it is lkj speaking in voices of the living & the dead
it is checking it out muta style
it is rasta ranting in benjamin
it is grandma's rocking chair rap from a broken lap
it is the lion's roar in grandpa's grey snore
it is baby's dummy tit microphone
it is for all ages living at all stages
it is papa ramps lighting all the lamps
it is that & more it is blood & gore
it is not scratching the sore it is just getting to the core
to get the pus to come to pass
it is taking rubber stamps from power clamps
it is DEMOCRACY beyond the statute book
it is rocking to the rhythm of the drum & the bass
it is pumping up the pace of the human race
it is a smile on the face of a mental case
it is sunrays beyond our sorry days
it is simply poetry ✓

tattered rain
& i'm navy blue
in the frayed streets
pressure reaching down
& slow magic coming on
drum flute & the night whistle
mute music of torn throats

& then . . .
tongues twisted around on themselves
spew out froth
green
rabid at yellow dusk . . .

& the night gathers its red soaked apparel
staggers home

Seitlhamo Motsapi

SHAK-SHAK

& the carnival entered the last streets
of the shantytown of

my soul // lightning speed rhythm
light moving heavy swinging hip

& so the poor wd throw pots of paint
curdled in the heart to the drowsy skies

so the portraits wd sprout, paint
of our joy colouring the clouds

riotous multicolour, righteous marching
shak-shak prophet majaja in front

riotous bell & thundering drum
shak-shak mthembu foot

sore from his impatient corns

& the carnival entered the last street
shack shack landscape grey

hunger a mere sunshine away / & yet
& yet the joy – profuse like air

mirth in madness, spirits rejoicing

& so the madmen – the high
voltage jolly demons, feet

shoo shoo shifty snap shuffle

& so the merry madmen of my soul

had the season's last stomp
after the chafe & bruise
of the 8 to 5 tortures

& while the electrick carnival
  kicked the weals off
  for the redeemer

already there's a sign
in the sky
for those who see

already the graffiti's up
the walls of my soul:

HISTRYS ON DE SIDE
OF DE OPRES

ENIA

my love is like a river or a fist with forty fingers
my love is like a river that swallows mirrors & saxophones
& spits out the purple pink salt of songs without heads
while the skies dance like loa grandmothers

my love is a forty-headed fist
sated on the scented innards of mediocrities
that smile like overdressed rainbows
while temples run into my frenzied wounds
my love is like a road that has grown wings
travellers drum their contemptible corrosions
up the walls of my head
that spits out the tasteless feet of nomads

my love growls softly slow into a child
or a knot of long-legged affirmations
tranquil & ray-banned like ancestor khoisan
against the boiling wiles of the sun
that is silent like the battered death
that sleeps on the skeleton coast
                    Mungu ndiye ajua kila kitu
                        the elders say

                    God is the one who knows everything
                    God is the one who knows everything

S O L / O

        my love
        there are no accidents
        in war – no kisses
        on the belligerent lips of crocodiles
        no loves greener than
        the dancing hearts of children
        no reveller jollier than the worm
        in columbus's boiling head

        there are no songs beautifuller
        than the stern indifference of the hills
        there are no flowers more clamorous
        than the seas of children
        home in my little heart

        i tell u this
        as the sun recedes
        into the quaking pinstripe
        of my warriors
        grinning & vulgar in their muddied dreams
        of power

299

i tell u this love
because the roads
have become hostile

MUSHI

tomorrow
they'll ask u
to renounce the skies
that throb in yr heart
like pregnant forests

they'll ask u
to spit at the blk doves
that hibernate in yr soul
while they wait
for the season of crosses & songs
for the season of loves that sigh
like contrite infernos

& while
coca-cola boils on the tongues
of their bloated preachers
& typhoons kiss their tottering empires
death & dollars stacked in their intestines

while zealots & faggots hunt u
so the Machine can piss
on the temples of the world's poor

i cave u sanctuaries
in the belly of my vengeant fire
i glue yr name
on the calm mouth of my hasty machete

child
there is hope yet
as the hills call out
yr name that gives birth to suns
& to music

there is hope yet
as we feed fire
into our stride

there is hope yet
as we remember
to roll back the blood
& mutilate the beast
who brought us mirrors & darkness

THE SUN USED TO BE WHITE

now since blkness can be a betrayal or
a shuttling blaze of glory rending the sky

since blkness can be a metaphor for deprivation
or a drumming beyond the shackle & the shove
created blk like vengeant spears
& greeting the sun in outstretched arms
where blk was the colour & caress of abysses
where blk was the razor clamour of inner decay
& meaning spat at us high white & dry
like an ache over kiliminjaro
the scowl of the sun & the sneer of the skies
lacerating mah history into a scarred holler

i was learning the sulphur smile of sneers
i was learning the jagged jig of fire

blood knotting into hate like the tall hearts
of ancestor maasai
melting into the purple nikon pose
of tourorist disca/dence
while herds slink into mouths of nairobi daggers
or the neon surfeit of bloo-eyed yoo-wes sailors
who can't get enough of mombassa's ochre thighs

we was born blk in a time & planet
where blk petered into absences & voids
where blk was the disco/dant melody
of the primal song of emptiness
that preceded rainbows & guerillas
a bleeding emptiness that burned mysteries
into the shallow hearts of feelanthropists
or a hasty scythe in the staccato palms
of mau mau gentlemen
with eyes like careless sharks
& hearts impatient like stubborn prophets

i was stumbling upon the rock of onelessness
up over the precipice where handshakes
triple hastily into hammers or typhoons
so the rampant slow kwashiorkor
of my histri books cd learn mud & manners
so the worm dancing cosy behind the razor wire
& the flooding blood in my i-eye cd learn
the sugar of winds & whips like all of us

in my head guerillas ecstatic
like storms or ash
it was biko like a yell of crosses
preaching deliverance from up on housetops
lov to sprout blk & concrete compassion
from the festered cracks on the faces of slaves
from the punctured hearts of my loved ones

in my head
it was gahvi rolling hills & hurling boulders
over lies & cries
while in my heart amerikkka shrieked
her rotting din of deceit & conceit
her long fangs singing into rapine orgies
gahvi was a star rising over depths
chains & murder a ready skulk
as our hearts began the sure dance
of burning spears

for the masterplan is not a flag or two
up the invisible masts of rebirths
it's more than the solid pre-harmony
of shrieks & screams
as we holler our thunder over the wounds
it's not the comical contentedness
of your own bucketful of the ocean
love is in the receding wave of the heart
the cool slink from the rainbow
into the embrace of the mesenja

& though the ocean clamours into a roar
 though the waters invoke the drowsy spirit
of thunder
        the ocean is very shallow
        a time short like loss
        a mountain low like hate
the ocean is very shallow

MISSA JOE

all jegged & tie
he forgets smiles & rivers
he forgets the ancient sugar of handshake

303

while his name slumps into sneer snarl
monosyllabic fester cripple
of dragon snore gripple

i offer him
the deep dizzying water of respects
from the hills & the herds
but he barks into the weary puddle
of offich inglish & boss shittish

so now
the purple of his rubber stabs
grows into a wall
but the drums won't fall asleep
    the drums won't fall asleep

RIVER ROBERT

we are at peace here
even while our lungs are full
of secret wars
& primordial fears bruise our suns
we are at peace here robert

with hopes upon our heads
& songs sprouting out of our sins
we bless the lacerations

we are at peace here
across the rock & scrub
a sole rainbow pillar
protrudes from the earth, full
of promise & solace

304

i have one eye full of dreams & hintentions
the other is full of broken mirrors
& cracked churchbells

i have one eye full of rivers & welcomes
the other is full of flickers & fades

i have
a memory full of paths & anointings
a mouth full of ripe infant suns
seven legs for the dancing river & the clement abyss
& a hope that corrodes the convulsions

we bless the long rough road
we bless the inscrutable darkness
where our names are rent into spirit
we bless the splinters & the air
full of asphyxiations & amnesia
we bless our lacerations & our deformities

we bless the belligerent strangers
who stay on in our throats
long after forgotten festivities

as we learn the painful lessons of love
as we learn to respect the night's sovereignty
& the slow stern wisdom of the desert
we bless the mysteries & the silence

This appendix provides an approximate idea of the years in which the poems in this anthology were first published. An asterisk indicates the year in which a poem was either written or published in a literary journal or anthology; the remaining dates refer to publication in a book by the poet.

With the exception of four poems, all the work in this volume appeared after 1960, the year of the Sharpeville massacre as well as the banning of the African National Congress and the Pan-Africanist Congress. The poems in question ("After the Riot" and "Within" by Sydney Clouts, "The Land of the People Once Living," by Sob. W. Nkuhlu, and "The Contraction and Enclosure of the Land" by St. J. Page Yako) seem to me to fit in with the prevalent, oppressive mood of the 1960s. More generally, the poetry of the 1950s and before was not taken into account in making this selection.

Section I

Stephen Watson: All poems are "versions" of 1870s narratives published in 1991.

Sydney Clouts: Firebowl (1966); Hotknife (1966); Stick Song (1966); North Wind (1960*); Within (1956*); After the Riot (1954*); Poetry Is Death Cast Out (1961*).

Ingrid Jonker: "I went searching for the way of my body . . . " (1963); Tokoloshe (1966); Bitterberry Daybreak (1963); Pregnant Woman (1963); Homesickness for Cape Town (1966); The Child Who Was Shot Dead by Soldiers in Nyanga (1963).

Sob. W. Nkuhlu: The Land of the People Once Living (1956).

St. J. Page Yako: The Contraction and Enclosure of the Land (1958).

Dennis Brutus: Nightsong: City (1963); Cold (1968).

Arthur Nortje: Waiting (1967*).

Adam Small: Come, Let Us Sing (1962); Great Krismis Prayer (1962); Preacher (1962); On the P'rade (1962); Gesondheid! (1962); Black Bronze Beautiful (1975).

Section II

Mongane Wally Serote: Alexandra (1972); City Johannesburg (1971*); I Will Wait (1972); Ofay-Watcher Looks Back (1972); For Don M. – Banned (1974); Milk and Corn (1974); Hell, Well, Heaven (1972*); No Baby Must Weep (1975).

Breyten Breytenbach: "I will die and go to my father . . . " (1976); my heritage (1984); "how drowsy we were wrapped in coolness . . . " (1972); the truth (1984); plagiarism (1976); december (1984); for Françooi Viljoen (1985).

Wopko Jensma: Spanner in the What? Works (1975*); Cry Me a River (1974); Our King (1973); My Hands (1972*); Confidentially Yours (1973); Now That It's Too Late (1974); My Brother (1973); Joburg Spiritual (1968*).

Eva Bezwoda: "A tooth dressed up in jackboots . . . " (1973); "Sometimes the mouth's a locked cell . . . " (1973); The Bullet (before 1976); Villages (before 1976); Ice Floes (before 1976); "He lay with her . . . " (1973).

Njabulo S. Ndebele: Be Gentle (1971*); The Revolution of the Aged (1980*); The Man of Smoke (1973*).

Mbuyiseni Oswald Mtshali: Boy on a Swing (1968*); Men in Chains (1971); Amagoduka at Glencoe Station (1972); The Detribalised (1971); Talismans (1981).

Mandla Langa: The Pension Jiveass (1971*).

Mazisi Kunene: Death of the Miners or The Widows of the Earth (1982); The Political Prisoner (1974); The Tyrant (1987*); A Note to All Surviving Africans (1987*); To My Friend Solomon Hailu (1996*).

Sheila Cussons: Clothed Nakedness (1978); Organ (1981); The Barn-Yard (1978); Yellow Gramophone (1981); Pearl (1970).

Wilma Stockenström: Africa Love (1970); East Coast (1973); Koichab's Water (1973); The Rock (1970); Confession of a Glossy Starling (1976); The Skull Laughs though the Face Cries (1976); Housebreaking of the Mamba (1970).

Jeni Couzyn: Christmas in Africa (1975).

Section III

Oupa Thando Mthimkulu: Like a Wheel (1978*); Nineteen Seventy-Six (1978*).

Motshile Nthodi: Staffrider (1978); South African Dialogue (1976*).

K. Zwide: Wooden Spoon (1979*).

Sipho Sepamla: Da Same, Da Same (1975*).

Mafika Gwala: Gumba, Gumba, Gumba (1971*); Bonk'abajahile (1978*); Kwela-Ride (1970*); Tap-Tapping (1979*); One Small Boy Longs for Summer (1977).

Chris van Wyk: It Is Sleepy in the 'Colored' Townships (1979); Candle (1979); The Road (1987*); We Can't Meet Here, Brother (1978*); In Detention (1979); A Riot Policeman (1979).

Peter Horn: The Eruption of Langa, 30th March 1960 (1979).

Stephen Gray: Local History (1982); The Song of the Gold Coming In (1979).

Patrick Cullinan: To Have Love (1984); The First, Far Beat (1984); The Dust in the Wind (1984); North (1965*); Sir Tom (1986); Etruscan Girl (1989).

Don Maclennan: Letters (1990*); "Winter sunlight, clean as a cut orange . . . " (1995); Funeral III (1995).

Douglas Livingstone: Gentling a Wildcat (1970); A Piece of Earth (1978); Mpondo's Smithy, Transkei (1978).

Section IV

Jeremy Cronin: "To learn how to speak . . . " (1983); "Our land holds . . . " (1983); White Face, Black Mask (1983); Poem-Shrike (1983); *Motho ke Motho ka Batho Babang* (1983); Walking on Air (1983); I Saw Your Mother (1983); Your Deep Hair (1983).

Gcina Mhlophe: The Dancer (1987*).

Douglas Reid Skinner: The Body Is a Country of Joy and Pain (1987*); Law and Order (1987*).

Donald Parenzee: The Raining (1985); Interview (1985); Changes at the Settlement (1992*).

Andries Walter Oliphant: Childhood in Heidelberg (1988*); Poem for My Mother (1988); After Life (1991*); Song of the Unemployed (1982*); The Hunger Striker (1989*); Blue (1994*).

Ingrid de Kok: Small Passing (1988); Our Sharpeville (1988); Sun, Aloe, Rain (1983*); To Drink Its Water (1988); This Thing We Learn from Others (1988); Brush Stroke (1992*); Inner Note (1990*); Ground Wave (1994*).

Stephen Watson: North-West Cape, 1985 (1986); Descending, Late (1995).

Phil du Plessis: Easter Transit (1986).

Petra Müller: Foretelling (1990*).

Antjie Krog: Ma (1970); Song of the Cyclists (1972); a one-dimensional song for the northern free state, more specifically middenspruit (1985); lovesong after the music of K. E. Ntsane (1985); "I don't glance at your grizzled hair . . . " (1985); transparency of the sole (1989); refused march at Kroonstad Monday 23 Oct 1989 (1995); land (1995).

Karen Press: Disposed Words (1991*); Tikolosh (1989*); Statues (1994*); Heart's Hunger (1991*); Needlework (1992*); The First Thirty-Seven Years (1995*); Can't Stand, Can't Dance (1993*); Tiresias in the City of Heroes (1994*).

Robert Berold: Dark City (1989); Two Meditations on Chuang Tsu (1988*); Praise Poem (1984); There Is a River in Me (1984*); meet me (1993*); Those Days (1996*).

Kelwyn Sole: Poem from Botswana (1977*); Presence (1989*); Mankunku (1985*); The National Question (1992); Woman, Trespassing in a Garden (1991*); Homecoming (1995*); Housing Targets (1995*).

Section V

Tatamkhulu Afrika: Tamed (1994*); The Funeral of Anton Fransch (1990*); The Trap (1990*); The Mugging (1992*); Who Were You? (1992); Cat on a High Yard Wall (1991); Remembering (1990*); Solitary Child (1995); Nightrider (1991*).

Joan Metelerkamp Sunday Night – On My Own – After the Uitenhage Shootings (1992); Trees Sky Space (1995); Dove (1996).

Lisa Combrinck: Ghazal (1994*); In the Moonlight (1994*).

Cathy Zerbst. Magnolia Blue (1995*).

Johann de Lange· Koos Prinsloo [1957–1994] (1995).

Ari Sitas. Evening Tides I (1989), Ethekwini (1989), Slave Trades (1993*).

Sandile Dikeni: Track of the Tracks (1994*)

Rustum Kozain· Family Portrait (1993*), Brother, Who Will Bury Me? (1995*).

Mxolisi M Nyezwa· barracks (1992*), things change (1989*), I cannot think of all the pains (1996*)

Lesego Rampolokeng· After Bra W's Flowers (1993); In Transition (1993); For the Oral (1992*); Wet pain . . tread with care (1994*).

Seitlhamo Motsapi: shak-shak (1995); enia (1994*); sol/o (1994*); mushi (1992*), the sun used to be white (1993*); missa joe (1995); river robert (1994*).

1. People

Biko, Steve An emblematic leader of the Black Consciousness Movement, killed in custody in 1977

Cetshwayo: Zulu king de facto from 1856 (formally from 1872) to 1879, the year the British finally crushed the Zulu army

Dingaan or Dingane Zulu king from the late 1820s until 1840 Dingaan's Day (now called Day of Reconciliation) celebrates the Afrikaner victory at Blood River (see Places and Historical Events)

Don M · Don Mattera, political activist and writer whose work was banned in the early 1970s for a duration of eight and a half years

Dumile Dumile Feni, a sculptor who rose to prominence in the 1960s An active sympathizer of the banned African National Congress, he was finally forced into exile.

Fransch, Anton: A young soldier who fought for Umkhonto we Sizwe (armed wing of the African National Congress) in the Western Cape in the mid-1980s. Fully armed in what he thought was a safe house, he held off a heavy police barrage for several hours, he was eventually killed when the police blew up the house.

Mankunku: Mankunku Ngozi, saxophone player.

Mhlakaza Father of the young Xhosa girl Nomquasi, whose nineteenth-century apocalyptic vision led her people to kill all their cattle and burn all their grain

Mrs Ples. Early Australopithicus Africus skull (2–3 million years old) discovered by Robert Broom in the Sterkfontein Caves

Prinsloo, Koos: Afrikaans writer, born in Kenya, who died of AIDS

Sobukwe, Robert: Founder of Pan-Africanist Congress in 1959.

Thoko Thoko Mcinga, a popular singer of the late 1960s

Tilane. A great Sotho warrior

Tiro, Abraham A black student leader, forced into exile and killed by a letter bomb in the early 1970s.

Viljoen, Françooi: François Villon.

2. Places and Historical Events

Alexandra. One of the oldest black townships, on the outskirts of Johannesburg

Bekkersdal: A town in Northwest Province where state violence was directed at the black community in the late 1980s

Blood River. Formerly the Ncane River On 16 December 1838, Afrikaners trekking into the hinterland won a decisive battle there against a Zulu army

Boipatong Black township in the Vaal Triangle, scene of intense violence in the early 1990s.

Bonteheuwel: "Coloured" township to which inhabitants of District Six were moved by force.

Bullhoek (*or* Bulhoek): Village in the Eastern Cape where the police and army shot members of a religious community in 1922

Chwannisberg. Johannisberg.

District Six: "Coloured" township in Cape Town, proclaimed a "white" area and razed to the ground in the late 1960s; now a wasteland.

Empangeni. A town in KwaZulu-Natal where state violence was directed at the black community in the late 1980s.

the Fort: A prison in Johannesburg.

Hacumqua: One of the Khoi tribes.

Igoli (*or* Egoli): City of Gold, Zulu name for Johannesburg

Inhaca: An island off the Mozambique coast.

Jo'burg, Joh'burg, Johannisberg. Johannesburg.

Kaoho: A village in Namibia

Karoo, Karroo. Semi-desert region in the Cape.

Katlehong: Black township on the East Rand, the scene of intense violence in the early 1990s.

Kgalagadi. The Kalahari desert

Koichab: Water source for Luderitz, a town in Namibia.

Langa: Black township outside Cape Town.

Makadas: Name given to the mainline train by the black residents of Victoria West (Northern Cape)

Masai Mara Kenya's most popular National Reserve.

1976: Year of the revolt by schoolchildren in Soweto and elsewhere, focused on state language policy in black schools. There were hundreds of casualties, though exact figures remain unknown.

Omundjavaira: A place in Namibia

Robben Island: Prison island where many black male political prisoners were incarcerated

Sharpeville: Black township in the Vaal Triangle, scene of a large protest against the "pass" laws in March 1960; sixty-nine people were killed and many wounded (see *dompas* in Glossary)

312

Sophiatown: Black township in Johannesburg, razed to the ground in the late 1950s

Treason Trial· From December 1956 to March 1961, opponents of apartheid, including Nelson Mandela, were charged with "high treason and conspiracy to use violence to overthrow the state," crimes punishable by death The accused were discharged

Uitenhage A town in the Eastern Cape where state violence was directed at the black community in the late 1980s

amagoduka: migrant labourer, lit. "returning ones" who go home at regular intervals (Zulu)

amaphela: cockroach (Zulu)

baas: boss; also sir, master (Afrikaans)

baasboy: boss boy, a black man given authority over his fellows by his white superiors

bazalwane: believers, especially Christian believers (Zulu)

biya: father

blaadjies: cigarette papers (Afrikaans)

bliksem: scoundrel (Afrikaans)

boer-boon tree: *Schotia*, evergreen flowering tree, lit. farmer-bean tree, with edible seeds

boetie: pal (lit. little brother) (Afrikaans)

Bolander: person from the Boland, wine region in the Western Cape (Afrikaans)

bonk'abajahile: everyone is in a hurry (Zulu)

bra: brother (diminutive)

braaivleis: barbecue (Afrikaans)

buchu (*or* bugu, boegoe): wild herb, any of several species of *Rutaceae*, used for medicinal purposes

casspir: armoured police van

"Coloured": South African of racially mixed descent

dagga: marijuana (Afrikaans)

dassie: rock rabbit (Afrikaans)

dik-dik: very small buck found mainly in Namibia (onomatopoeia, from call)

dompas (*or* pass): colloquial for the internal passport which all people except whites were obliged to carry (lit. stupid pass) (Afrikaans)

donga: small ravine, caused by soil erosion (Nguni)

dorp: country town (Afrikaans)

duwweltjie: thorn (Afrikaans)

eMalangeni: ancestry through the matrilineal line (Zulu). In cosmological terms, this implies a state of innocence.

fontein: fountain (Afrikaans)

fynbos: Cape coastal vegetation type consisting of numerous kinds of plants, many with narrow leaves (Afrikaans)

Gesondheid!: Cheers! (Afrikaans)

goeters: things (Afrikaans)

golovan: small tip trolley on rails, used to transport ore, etc., in the mines

gom-gom: musical instrument, similar to the gorah

gorah: African harp (poss. Nama)

guava: fruit, but also vulgarism referring to female genitals

gumba: dance party

gumba-gumba: ghetto blaster

gwarrie (*or* ghwarrie, guarri): *Euclea ondulata,* a shrub with succulent fruit

hamba kahle: go well (Zulu), a farewell greeting

hayikona (*or* aikona): emphatic negative, "Not on your life!" (Nguni)

hippo: armored police vehicle

ikwata bust fife: a quarter past five

inkululeko: lit. freedom, here used as the name of a workers' newspaper (Zulu)

jiveass: imponderable hurdle (black American slang)

July Handicap: annual Durban horse race

Khoikhoi: see Khoisan

Khoisan: the aboriginal non-Bantu-speaking inhabitants of South Africa. Colloq. Hottentot (Khoi, pastoralist) and Bushman (San, hunter-gatherer)

khotla (*or* kgotla): tribal meeting place, also tribal court (Tswana)

Kleeling: "Coloured" (see ref.) (Afrikaans)

kleinbaas: young boss (Afrikaans)

kokerboom: large aloe, *Aloe dichotoma* (Afrikaans)

kuil: pool or hole (Afrikaans)

kukumakranka: khoikhoi name for *Gethyliss afra,* a delicate starlike Cape lily yielding an aromatic edible fruit

kwela: township pennywhistle music

kwela-kwela: police van

lobola: dowry, usually in cattle (Nguni)

location: township area of black, "Coloured," or Indian habitation, situated outside a white town or city

majita: guy, buddy (tsotsitaal, i.e., gangster slang)

makgala: aloes (Sotho)

Malombo: a jazz idiom combining tribal rhythms with urban jazz

mathangan'abomvu: red thighs, possibly referring to light-skinned women (Zulu)

mayibuye Afrika (*or* mayibuy'i Afrika): Come back Africa; rallying cry of the African National Congress (Nguni)

"maximum": Pretoria maximum security prison

mbaqanga: in the 1950s, term used for popular jazz that blended African melody, marabi, and American jazz; in the 1960s, term used to designate a new music combining urban neotraditional music and marabi

meerkat (*or* mierkat): suricate, a Southern African burrowing mongoose (Afrikaans)

meths: methylated spirits

moegie (or moogie, mugu, moegoe): a sucker or country bumpkin (black urban slang)

mohlalefi: one who knows everything (Sotho)

mokgatjane: meeting of tribal elders (Sotho)

mqombothi: traditional beer brewed from sorghum (Zulu)

mzalwane: singular of bazalwane

nyanga (or inyanga): traditonal healer (Zulu)

otsogile: how are you? (Tswana)

palmiet: *Prionium,* a type of bulrush (Afrikaans)

phansi: down (Zulu)

pondok: shack, hovel (Afrikaans)

rhebok (or reebok): roebuck (Afrikaans)

ringhals (or rinkals): ring-necked cobra

robot: traffic light

San: see Khoisan

sayibek'apha: we put it here (Xhosa)

sayithath'apha: we take it here (Xhosa)

sdudla sibomvu: fat red girl, probably referring to the fact that she is light-skinned (Zulu)

shebeen: illegal bar or drinking den

sishov'ingolovane: we push the tip trolley (see golovan). This Zulu phrase is the title of a hit song by the group Stimela.

skollie: hooligan (Afrikaans)

smokkel: smuggle (Afrikaans)

sojikel'emaweni, sojikela'aphi na he: I'll go off to some distant land, where can we find direction in our journey? Lines from a famous song by Miriam Makeba (Xhosa)

songololo: millipede (Zulu)

staffrider: person who rides illegally on the outside of a suburban train

steenbokkie: local species of ibex (Afrikaans)

stoep: stoop, porch or verandah in front of or all around a house (Afrikaans)

stompie: cigarette butt (Afrikaans)

tambuti: rare indigenous tree used for making furniture

tjhutjhumakgala: train

tokoloshe (*or* tikolosh): an evil, virile dwarflike spirit within the African belief system

tot: labourers, particularly on wine farms, receive part of their wages in "tots" of wine

tsena: come in (Tswana)

velschoen (*or* velskoen): rawhide shoe (Afrikaans)

vetkoek: a fritter usually made of yeast dough (Afrikaans)

vlei: swamp or pond (Afrikaans)

vygie: generic name for an indigenous plant, *Mesembryanthemum* (Afrikaans)

Wa sala wena: You, stay! (Zulu)

Welcome Dover: stove (brand)

wildebeest: gnu (Afrikaans)

wrinkals: see ringhals

xhegwazana phek'ipapa: old woman, cook cornmeal porridge. From a traditional children's song (Xhosa).

zol: marijuana cigarette

Tatamkhulu Afrika. Born in Sollum, Egypt, in 1920. The son of an Arab father and a Turkish mother, he was brought to South Africa in 1923 He was a prisoner of war for three years in Italy and Germany, after which he worked off and on for twenty years in the Namibian copper mines. He settled in Cape Town in the 1960s, converted to Islam, and joined the resistance to apartheid Arrested in 1987 for "terrorism," he was listed for five years as a banned person He has published two novels, a collection of novellas, and six volumes of poetry, including *Nine Lives* (1991), *Dark Rider* (1992), and *Maqabane (Comrade)* (1994)

Robert Berold was born in Johannesburg in 1948. For most of his working life he has been involved in rural development, at one point editing a technical resource manual for rural communities Since 1984 he has been involved with the Power Station, a handcraft development centre in Grahamstown In 1989 he became editor of the poetry journal *New Coin,* publishing in it much of the innovative poetry that has been written in the country since that time. He is the author of two collections of poems *The Door to the River* (1984) and *The Fires of the Dead* (1989)

Eva Bezwoda was born in Vienna in 1942, arriving in South Africa at the age of eight She taught English and German at the University of Natal, and was involved in Renoster Books in the early 1970s, helping to publish the first books by Mtshali and Serote. *One Hundred and Three Poems* (1973) records the inner struggle that led to her suicide in 1976 *Poems* was published posthumously in 1994

Breyten Breytenbach. Born in Bonnievale, Western Cape, in 1939 He lived in Paris from 1961 to 1975, when he entered South Africa illegally for political purposes, only to be arrested and imprisoned for seven years of a nine-year sentence He now divides his time between South Africa, France, and Spain A painter as well as a writer, he has been a strong reference point for South African, and more particularly Afrikaans, writers over the past three decades He has published at least fifteen volumes of poetry in Afrikaans. Several selections exist in English, including *In Africa Even the Flies Are Happy* (1978), *And Death . . White as Words* (1978), and *Judas Eye* (1988). In addition, he has written two collections of short stories, short prose pieces, novels, essays, and three autobiographical accounts of his travels and prison experience in South Africa

Dennis Brutus. Born in Salisbury, Rhodesia, of South African parents in 1924 Educated at South African universities, he taught at high schools until he was banned from all gatherings in 1961 He served a term of eighteen months hard labour on Robben Island and a year under house arrest before emigrating in 1966. As president of the South African Non-Racial Olympic Committee, he played a key role in the dismissal of South Africa and Rhodesia from the Olympic Games He has lived in the United States since 1983, teaching literature at Northwestern University and then the University of Pittsburgh His books of poetry include *Sirens, Knuckles, Boots* (1962), *Letters to Martha and Other Poems from a South African Prison* (1968), and *A Simple Lust* (1973).

Sydney Clouts. Born in Cape Town in 1926, he worked there as an editor and contributed to the founding of the literary journal *Contrast*. He emigrated to Britain with his family in 1961. Apart from a two-year research fellowship in South Africa, he continued to live in Britain, where he worked as a librarian until his death in 1982. An influential volume of poems, *One Life*, was published in 1966. *Collected Poems* followed posthumously in 1984.

Lisa Combrinck Born in Cape Town in 1967, she has worked as a journalist for *The Southern African Review of Books* and *South,* and served on the national executive committee of the Congress of South African Writers. She lectures in English at Vista University in the township of Mamelodi. A selection of her poems, "The Shadow of Desire," appeared in the 1992 anthology *Essential Things,* edited by Andries Walter Oliphant

Jeni Couzyn was born in Johannesburg in 1942. She studied at the University of Natal and taught drama both in Soweto and Rhodesia. In 1965 she emigrated to Britain, where she made a living out of poetry before becoming a psychotherapist She has written books for children, and edited three poetry anthologies. Her own poems have been published in six collections, including *Christmas in Africa* (1975) and *In the Skin House* (1993). Her selected poems, *Life by Drowning,* appeared in expanded form in 1985.

Jeremy Cronin was born in Simonstown, Western Cape, in 1949, and studied philosophy at the University of Cape Town and the Sorbonne. He lectured in Cape Town before being convicted under the Terrorism Act for working with the African National Congress. He was jailed for seven years; his collection of poems, *Inside,* was published the year of his release, 1983. Since that time, he has lectured in philosophy and worked for the United Democratic Front Currently assistant general secretary of the South African Communist Party, he also heads its publications department

Patrick Cullinan. Born in Pretoria in 1932 After an education in England, he farmed and ran a sawmill in the Eastern Transvaal He cofounded Bateleur Press, was founder-editor of the literary magazine *The Bloody Horse,* and has lectured in literature at the University of the Western Cape Four collections of poetry, including *Today Is Not Different* (1978) and *The White Hail in the Orchard and Other Poems* (1984), have been followed by his *Selected Poems 1961–1994*

Sheila Cussons was born near Piketberg in the Western Cape in 1922, of Afrikaans and Irish parents. She lived in Spain for twenty-five years before returning to South Africa in 1982, and works in Cape Town as a graphic artist. She has published essays, a translation of Borges, and twelve volumes of poetry since 1970, including *Die Heilige Modder (The Holy Mire)* (1986) and *Die Knetterende Woord (The Crackling Word)* (1990) In 1985 she published *Poems,* a selection of poems in English, which she herself translated from the Afrikaans.

Ingrid de Kok. Born in Johannesburg in 1951, she grew up in Stilfontein, a mining town in the Western Transvaal. She studied in South Africa and Canada, and directs the Department of Adult Education and Extra Mural Studies at the University of Cape Town. Her poems have been collected in the volume *Familiar Ground*, published in 1988. She coedited *Spring Is Rebellious Arguments about Cultural Freedom* (1990) and was advisory editor for the *World Literature Today* issue on South African literature (1996).

Johann de Lange was born in Pretoria in 1959, and studied Afrikaans and literary theory at the University of Pretoria and the University of South Africa. He currently teaches a creative writing class at the University of Cape Town and is on the editorial staff of the literary magazine *Ensovoort (And So Forth)*. His English translations of Afrikaans poems have appeared in several publications. Apart from a recent collection of short stories, he has published seven books of Afrikaans poetry, including *Akwarelle van die Dors (Aquarelles of Thirst)* (1993) and *Wat Sag is Vergaan (That which Is Soft Perishes)* (1995)

Sandile Dikeni. Born in Victoria West, Northern Cape, in 1966, he began writing seriously while in detention for political reasons in 1986. He has worked as a journalist for *Die Suid Afrikaan* and the *Cape Times*, and currently produces a weekly radio programme on the Truth and Reconciliation Commission. His collection of poems, *Guava Juice* (slang for Molotov cocktail), was published in 1992

Phil du Plessis was born in Fouriesburg, in the Orange Free State, in 1944. He works as a medical practitioner and psychotherapist near Cape Town. He was founding editor of the literary journal *Wurm*, and editor of the magazines *New Nation* and *Izwi*, which launched a number of prominent black writers. Apart from a volume of translations of Han Shan, he has published seven volumes of poetry, including *Openbaringe en Johannes (Revelations and St. John)* (1992), *Engel uit die Paradys (Angel out of Paradise)* (1994), and *Nagjoernaal (Nightjournal)* (1996).

Stephen Gray. Born in Cape Town in 1941; educated at the University of Cape Town, Cambridge, and the Iowa Writers' Workshop. He lectured in literature at the Rand Afrikaans University in Johannesburg for many years, becoming head of the department, and took early retirement in 1991. His extensive concern for the world of South African letters is shown in numerous critical works; *South African Literature, an Introduction* was published in 1979. He has edited numerous anthologies of poetry and short stories, and written novels, plays, short stories, and an autobiography. His six volumes of poetry include *Apollo Café and Other Poems* (1989) and *Taken* (1995). *Selected Poems (1960–1992)* was published in 1994.

Mafika Gwala was born in Verulam, Natal, in 1946. Among other occupations, he has worked as an industrial relations officer amongst black workers in the Hammarsdale area. In the early 1970s he was a leading exponent of the

Black Consciousness Movement, and in 1987 went to the University of Manchester to study politics and labour relations. He was a founding member of the Mpumalanga Arts Ensemble. His literary output includes numerous critical articles and essays as well as two volumes of poetry: *Jol'iinkomo (Bringing the cattle home to the safety of the kraal)* (1977) and *No More Lullabies* (1982). In 1991 he collaborated with Liz Gunner in editing and translating a selection of Zulu praise poems, *Musho.*

Peter Horn Born in Teplitz-Schoenau, Czechoslovakia, in 1934, educated in Germany and South Africa; currently professor of German at the University of Cape Town. His large critical output includes two volumes of essays on South African poetry. A number of his own poems were composed for and recited at anti-apartheid rallies. He has published six volumes of poems, including *Silence in Jail* (1979) and *An Axe in the Ice* (1993). *Poems 1964–1989* appeared in 1991.

Wopko Jensma was born in Ventersdorp, Transvaal, in 1939, and went to the Universities of Pretoria and Potchefstroom. He lived in Mozambique and worked as a teacher and graphic artist for the Botswana Information Department before returning to South Africa in 1971. For personal reasons, he took the unusual step of having himself reclassified as black. Said to be schizophrenic, in recent years he has been in and out of psychiatric hospitals; at present he lives in Johannesburg. His three volumes of poetry include work in English and Afrikaans, with snippets of Tswana and other languages, as well as woodcuts and collages. They are *Sing for Our Execution* (1973), *Where White Is the Colour, Where Black Is the Number* (1974), and *I Must Show You My Clippings* (1977).

Ingrid Jonker Born in 1933 in Douglas, near Kimberley, in the Northern Cape. She worked as a typist, secretary, and publisher's reader. Two collections of poetry in Afrikaans, *Ontvlugting (Escape)* in 1956 and *Rook en Oker (Smoke and Ochre)* in 1963, established her as a major, dissenting voice in Afrikaans lyric poetry before her death by suicide in 1965. A posthumous collection, *Kantelson (Setting Sun)* (1966), was followed by *Selected Poems* in English translation (1988).

Rustum Kozain was born in Paarl, Western Cape, in 1966. He is a prospective doctoral student in English literature at the University of Cape Town, where he tutors part time. In 1994–95 he spent ten months as a Fulbright student in the United States. A selection of his poems, *Desire for the Sun,* appeared in the 1992 anthology *Essential Things,* edited by Andries Walter Oliphant.

Antjie Krog was born in 1952 in Kroonstad, Orange Free State. She has worked as a teacher, lecturer, and editor, and in the 1980s openly engaged herself on the side of the African National Congress. She currently reports for Radio News on parliamentary affairs, and has also covered the proceedings of the Truth and Reconciliation Commission. Among her eight collections of

Afrikaans poems are *Jerusalemgangers* (*Jerusalemgoers*) (1985), *Lady Anne* (1989), and *Gedigte 1990–1995* (*Poems 1990–1995*).

Mazisi Ku was born in Durban, in 1930. He studied at Natal University before going into exile in 1959. He taught African languages and literature in Lesotho, London, and Los Angeles before returning to Natal University as a professor in the 1990s He was a founding member of the Anti-Apartheid Movement in Great Britain, representing the African National Congress in Europe and the United States Apart from his critical writings, he has contributed to the revival of Zulu poetry, translating several works into English These include epic poems and the volumes *Zulu Poems* (1970) and *The Ancestors and the Sacred Mountain,* the latter of which deals with Zulu religion and cosmology

Mandla Langa was born in Durban in 1950, and studied at Fort Hare University He left the country in 1976, and served the African National Congress in exile as an editor, speechwriter and cultural attaché He is currently president of the Congress of South African Writers and chairman of Thabo Mbeki's task group investigating the government's communications structure Apart from a few poems, he has published three novels and a collection of short stories, *The Naked Song* (1996) He is one of the first South African writers to give voice to the trauma accompanying return from exile

Douglas Livingstone was born in Kuala Lumpur, Malaysia, in 1932, and arrived in South Africa at the age of ten. He trained as a bacteriologist in Southern Rhodesia and settled in Durban in 1964, where he worked as a consultant microbiologist on the question of sea pollution The author of several radio plays, his seven volumes of poetry include *A Rosary of Bone* (1975, 1983), *The Anvil's Undertone* (1978), and *A Littoral Zone* (1991) His *Selected Poems* were published in 1984. He died in 1996.

Don Maclennan was born in London in 1929 and came to South Africa in 1938 He has spent most of his working life as a teacher both in South Africa and in the United States, retiring from Rhodes University after twenty-nine years there. Apart from a handful of scholarly works, he has published plays, short stories, and six collections of poems *Collecting Darkness* was published in 1988, *Letters* in 1992, *The Poetry Lesson* in 1995.

Joan Metelerkamp was born in Pretoria in 1956, and grew up in the Natal Midlands. She studied acting at the University of Cape Town, and has taught English at the Universities of the Western Cape and Natal She has published two collections of poetry, *Toeing the Line* (1991) and *Stone No More* (1995)

Gcina Mhlophe was born in Hammarsdale, Natal, in 1958. She has worked extensively in the theater—notably the Market Theatre, Johannesburg—as an actress and director. She has also worked for radio and television, and is a film actress In 1994, with Ladysmith Black Mambazo, she released an album of children's songs and stories, it is above all for the vitality of her storytelling that she has achieved renown Apart from children's tales and short stories for adults, she has published a play and a scattering of poems.

Seitlhamo Motsapi was born in 1966 in Bela Bela, a township outside Warmbaths in the Northern Transvaal. He studied at the University of the Witwatersrand and the University of the North, where he now lectures in English His first volume of poetry, *earthstepper/the ocean is very deep,* was published in 1995

Oupa Thando Mthimkulu was born in 1952 in Petrus Steyn, Orange Free State. He published poems in *Staffrider* magazine in the late 1970s and continues to write poetry as well as plays He lives in Soweto.

Mbuyiseni Oswald Mtshali was born in KwaBhanya, near Vryheid, Natal, in 1960. He was working as a messenger in Johannesburg when his collection of poems, *Sounds of a Cowhide Drum,* was published in 1971; this book, which speaks of black experience in a way few had done previously, had unusual success Since then he has studied at Columbia and New York Universities, and has worked as principal of a commercial college in Soweto and director of communications for the South African Council of Churches. A second volume of poems, *Fireflames,* appeared in 1980. He has also translated *Romeo and Juliet* into Zulu

Petra Müller, born in 1935, grew up in Swellendam in the Western Cape. After studying at Stellenbosch University, she worked as a fiction editor and features writer for *Sarie* magazine, then as a publishing editor. She is now a freelance journalist and lives on a farm on the Piketberg mountain range. She has published a children's story and some poems in English, but most of her writing—short stories for adults and three volumes of poetry, including *Obool* (*Obol*) in 1977 and *Patria* in 1979—has been in Afrikaans.

Njabulo S. Ndebele. Born in 1948 in Western Native Township, outside Johannesburg, he holds degrees from the Universities of Botswana, Lesotho, Swaziland at Roma, Lesotho, and from the Universities of Cambridge and Denver He was pro-vice chancellor of the University of Lesotho until 1990, when, after a long absence, he returned to South Africa, taking up key positions at the University of the Witwatersrand and the University of the Western Cape He is at present principal and vice-chancellor of the University of the North Widely recognized for the short stories in *Fools* (1983) and his theoretical essays, some of them collected in *Rediscovery of the Ordinary* (1991), he began his writing life as a poet in the late 1960s when he was a prominent figure in the Black Consciousness movement.

Sob. W. Nkuhlu was born in Tsomo, Transkei, in 1924. After working for many years as a health officer in Durban, he lived in self-imposed exile in Zambia from 1960 until his death in 1990. Some of his Xhosa poetry, most of it still unpublished, appeared in the collection *Imvaba* (*Calabash*) (1956).

Arthur Nortje. Born in Oudtshoorn, Western Cape, in 1942 At Patterson High School, Port Elizabeth, he was greatly influenced by his English teacher, Dennis Brutus He went on to the University of the Western Cape and Jesus College, Oxford After two years of teaching in Canada and British Colombia, he returned to Oxford in 1970, dying the same year of an overdose of barbiturates. His poetry is collected in two posthumous volumes, *Lonely Against the Light* and *Dead Roots*, both published in 1973

Motshile Nthodi was born in Lady Selborne township near Pretoria in 1948. He studied fine arts in Paris and has exhibited graphic arts widely in South Africa His collection of poetry *From the Calabash, Poems and Woodcuts* was published in 1978

Mxolisi M. Nyezwa was born in 1967 in New Brighton township outside Port Elizabeth. He teaches part time, trying to save enough money to complete his medical studies. He is a founding member of the Imvaba Cultural Society, which provides an outlet for the creative energies of township youth A selection of his poems, *To Have No Art*, was published in the 1992 anthology *Essential Things*, edited by Andries Walter Oliphant.

Andries Walter Oliphant was born in 1958 in Heidelberg, Transvaal, of Afrikaans and English-speaking parents. Educated at the Universities of the Western Cape and Oregon, he formerly served as an editor of *Staffrider* magazine, and of the publishing house established by the Congress of South African Writers (COSAW), where he edited several anthologies of short stories and poetry. He is currently engaged in the formulation of new arts policy in South Africa; he also lectures in literary theory at the University of South Africa. The author of a play and a collection of short stories, he is also a painter His poetry is collected in the volume *At the End of the Day* (1988)

Donald Parenzee was born in Cape Town in 1948 and grew up in District Six, a "Coloured" area on the edge of the city, since demolished He studied at the University of Cape Town, and works as an architect for a community development project. Previously involved in cultural organizations opposed to apartheid, he now also teaches creative writing and organizes theatre productions A collection of his poems, *Driven to Work*, was published in 1985

Karen Press was born in Cape Town in 1956. She has worked in alternative education projects, helped to found a publishing collective, and is employed as an editor of fiction for young adults. She coedited *Spring Is Rebellious. Arguments about Cultural Freedom* She has also published several stories and four collections of poetry to date, including *This Winter Coming* (1986), *Bird Heart Stoning the Sea* (1990), and *History Is the Dispossession of the Heart* (1992).

Lesego Rampolokeng was born in Soweto in 1965. After dropping out of the University of the North, working for a few months on the stock exchange, and a brief but dissident period reciting praise poetry at political meetings, he has turned to performing his poetry with musicians such as Vusi Mahlasela and Patience Agbabi. In 1995 he collaborated as a poet with theatre director William Kentridge in the production of *Faustus in Africa*. His two collections to date are *Horns for Hondo* (1990) and *Talking Rain* (1993).

Sipho Sepamla was born in Krugersdorp, Transvaal, in 1932. He has worked as a teacher, as an editor of the literary journals *New Classic* and *S'ketsh,* and is now director of the Federated Union of Black Artists (FUBA), a Johannesburg center for the training of black artists. He has written plays, short stories, and novels; his poetry collections include *The Soweto I Love* (1977), *Children of the Earth* (1983), and *Selected Poems* (1984)

Mongane Wally Serote. Born in 1944 in Sophiatown, a township within the Johannesburg area, since destroyed. In 1969 he spent nine months in solitary confinement but was released without being charged. In 1979 he studied at the University of Columbia, then went to work at the Medu Arts Ensemble in Gaberone, Botswana. Seven years later he began working for the Department of Arts and Culture at the U K office of the African National Congress. He is currently a member of parliament and chairman of its Portfolio Committee for Arts, Culture, Language, Science and Technology, as well as head of the ANC Department of Arts and Culture in Johannesburg His poetry was pivotal in the revival of black writing in the 1970s. His collections include *Yakhal'inkomo (The cry of cattle at the slaughterhouse)* (1972) and *Tsetlo (Honey-bird)* (1974); four long poems published in book form range from *No Baby Must Weep* (1975) to *Third World Express* (1992). He has also published a novel and a book of essays.

Ari Sitas was born in 1952 in Limassol, Cyprus, growing up first there and then in Johannesburg, where he went to the University of the Witwatersrand. He was one of the founding members of the Junction Avenue Theatre Company. In 1983, while involved in Durban trade union activities (particularly with COSATU, a federation of trade unions), he founded a workers' theatre movement, and directed and facilitated the development of grassroots plays He also edited the worker poetry book *Black Mamba Rising* (1986). He now coordinates the Industrial and Labour Studies Centre at Natal University and is editor of the *South African Labour Bulletin* He has written a play, the libretto for a surrealist opera, a novella, a collection of poems, *Tropical Scars* (1989), and a series of poem-songs titled *Songs, Shoeshine and Piano* (1992)

Douglas Reid Skinner was born in 1949 in the Northern Cape town of Upington. He has worked as a computer consultant, moving to London, then to New York and San Francisco, in the early 1970s. On his return to Cape Town in the mid 1980s, he founded The Carrefour Press, which specialized in publishing the English poetry of the region. He also edited the country's oldest literary journal, *New Contrast,* as well as starting and editing *The South African Literary*

Review He returned to the United Kingdom in the early 1990s. Apart from his poetry translations from Hebrew and Italian, he has published four volumes of poetry, including *The House in Pella District* (1985), *The Unspoken* (1988), and *The Middle Years* (1993).

Adam Small was born in Wellington in the Western Cape in 1936 and studied at the University of the Western Cape and at Oxford. He returned to the University of the Western Cape to teach philosophy, and is currently head of the Department of Social Work there. His first three collections of poetry, for the most part in the Cape "Coloured" idiom, include *Kitaar My Kruis* (*Guitar My Cross*) in 1961 and *Oos Wes Tuis Bes District Ses* (*East West Home's Best District Six*) in 1973 In 1975, he published a book of quatrains in English, *Black Bronze Beautiful*. He has also written plays in both languages

Kelwyn Sole was born in Johannesburg in 1951, and studied at the Universities of the Witwatersrand and London. He worked in Botswana and Namibia, from which he was deported in 1989 under the Undesirable Aliens' Act He currently lectures in English at the University of Cape Town He was an editor of a literary magazine, *Donga,* and has written wide-ranging essays on South African literature and culture. His poetry is collected in *The Blood of Our Silence* (1988) and *Projections in the Past Tense* (1992).

Wilma Stockenström was born in 1933 in Napier, Western Cape. She studied at the University of Stellenbosch and has worked as an actress and translator; she now lives in Cape Town She has written a play and five novels, including *Expedition to the Boabab* (English version 1983), with a density bordering on poetry Her first collection of poems, *Vir die Bysiende Leser* (*For the Near-Sighted Reader*) (1970), has been followed by five others, including *Spieel van Water* (*Mirror of Water*) (1973) and *Van Vergtelheid en van Glans* (*Of Oblivion and Lustre*) (1976)

Chris van Wyk Born in Johannesburg in 1957, he has worked for the educational trust SACHED, developing literacy materials, writing novels for children and teenagers, and recently editing a selection of readers' contributions to the youth magazine *Upbeat*. He cofounded the literary journal *Wietie* and edited the key literary journal *Staffrider* from 1981 to 1986 He has published short stories for adults and one volume of poetry, *It Is Time to Go Home* (1979).

Stephen Watson was born in 1954 in Cape Town, where he has lived almost all his life He is at present a lecturer in the English department at the University of Cape Town His poems are collected in *Poems 1977–83* (1983), *In This City* (1986), and *Cape Town Days* (1989). His celebrated "versions" of nineteenth-century /Xam narratives appeared in *Return of the Moon* (1991), reprinted as *Song of the Broken String* (1995).

St. J. Page Yako was born in Egokolweni, Transkei, in 1901, and worked as a teacher in the Eastern Cape His Xhosa poetry was published in two books,

Umtha Welanga (*Ray of the Sun*) and *Ikhwezi* (*Poems*), both in 1959. He died in 1977.

Cathy Zerbst was born in Bellville, Western Cape in 1959. She has been a singer, performing her own compositions in nightclubs for many years; she has also written music for the theatre and worked as a musical director. She now lives in Johannesburg, where she works as a managing editor for an educational publisher.

K. Zwide. Despite persistent research, nothing could be discovered about this poet, except that he or she published the poem "Wooden Spoon" in *Staffrider* 2, no. 3 (1979).